D0662344

THIS BOOK
BELONGS TO

A LITTLE GOD TIME FOR WOMEN

BroadStreet
PUBLISHING

BroadStreet Publishing Group LLC
Savage, Minnesota, USA
Broadstreetpublishing.com

A Little God Time for Women

ISBN 978-1-4245-5519-2 (faux)

Devotional entries composed by Janelle Anthony Breckell, Claire Flores, Cate Mezyk, Stephanie Sample, Jacquelyn Senske, and Michelle Winger.

Design by Chris Garborg | www.garborgdesign.com
Edited and compiled by Michelle Winger | www.literallyprecise.com
Cover and interior image © Bigstock/lozas

Printed in China.

18 19 20 21 7 6 5 4 3

THE LORD IS GOOD TO THOSE
WHOSE HOPE IS IN HIM,
TO THE ONE WHO SEEKS HIM;
IT IS GOOD TO WAIT QUIETLY
FOR THE SALVATION OF THE LORD.

LAMENTATIONS 3:25-26, NIV

INTRODUCTION

When everything else in life demands your attention, rest in the Lord to find the hope, joy, and peace you need each day.

This one-year devotional provides you with godly wisdom and insight to strengthen your faith and encourage your spirit.

The Father is captivated by you! He delights in every moment you choose to spend with him. Let your heart be filled with his presence and find the peace that is abundant there.

Be refreshed and inspired as you make *A Little God Time* part of your day.

You are so intimately aware of me, Lord.
You read my heart like an open book
and you know all the words I'm about to speak
before I even start a sentence!
You know every step I will take before my
journey even begins!

Psalm 139:3-4 TPT

SOMETHING NEW

Whether you have generated a color-coded list of goals, dreams, and an execution plan for the next 365 days or you've banned resolutions and vowed to make this just another day on the calendar, the clean slate represented by the first day of a new year is filled with an undeniable air of expectation. The excitement of a new bauble or gadget pales in comparison to the promise of a new beginning. Deep down inside, there is a part of us which thinks, "This could be my year!"

Guess what? It *is* your year. This day, and every one that follows, is yours. It is yours to choose who and how to love, to serve, and even to be. And the choice you made in reading this page represents the choice to take this journey in the company of your heavenly Father. That is a beautiful place to start.

> *"I am about to do something new.*
> *See, I have already begun! Do you not see it?*
> *I will make a pathway through the wilderness.*
> *I will create rivers in the dry wasteland"* (Isaiah 43:19, NLT).

What new thing would you like to do this year? What pathways do you need God to clear?

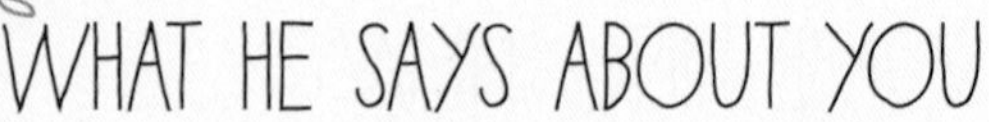

WHAT HE SAYS ABOUT YOU

In a memorable scene from a movie about teenage girls, a teacher asks a gymnasium full of young women to close their eyes and raise their hands if they've ever said anything bad about another girl. Virtually every hand is raised. The reason this scene rings true is that it *is* true. And sadly, we are often even harder on ourselves.

In addition to the amazing news that Mary would bear God's son, the angel who visits her in Luke 1 also tells Mary of her goodness, of her favor in God's eyes. Mary was a teenage girl. Chances are, she'd heard—and thought—something less than kind about herself on more than one occasion. Consider her brave, beautiful response:

> *Mary responded, "I am the Lord's servant. May everything you have said about me come true." And then the angel left her" (Luke 1:38, NLT).*

Are you self-critical? If asked to describe yourself, what would you say? Now think of someone who loves you. What do they say about you? Decide today to let their words—and God's words—be the truth. Join Mary in saying to God, "May everything you have said about me come true."

JANUARY 3

WHEN YOU FEEL STUCK

"Local authorities are reporting blizzard conditions on the Interstate…" Did your pulse just quicken, your muscles tense? No one likes to feel stuck, and blinding snow and unmoving vehicles on every side can cause even the most rational, laid-back woman to imagine leaping from her car and running over rooftops and across hoods, action hero style. What a fun way to test out the traction on your new winter boots. Or not. Anyway, stuck is stuck, right?

Maybe we feel stuck in our everyday lives. A job that doesn't utilize our gifts, a relationship that's more take than give, a habit that's edging toward addiction. Unlike that snow-covered freeway-turned-parking-lot, there is a direction to turn when circumstances have you feeling boxed in. Turn your face toward the Lord; let him fill you with the strength to move.

The Sovereign Lord is my strength! He makes me as surefooted as a deer, able to tread upon the heights (Habakkuk 3:19, NLT).

Where are you stuck right now? Professionally, personally, or perhaps in your prayer life, is there an area where you've simply stopped moving? Ask God for surefooted strength, and then go where he leads you.

THE FATHER'S LOVE

Regardless of how beautifully or how imperfectly your earthly father showed his love, your heavenly Father's love is utterly boundless. Rest in that thought a moment. There is nothing you can do to change how he feels about you. Nothing.

We spend so much time trying to make ourselves more lovable, from beauty regimens to gourmet baking, to being there for pretty much everyone. It's easy to forget we are already perfectly loved. Our Father loves us more than we can imagine. And he would do anything for us. *Anything.*

> *"If a man has a hundred sheep but one of the sheep gets lost, he will leave the other ninety-nine on the hill and go to look for the lost sheep. I tell you the truth, if he finds it he is happier about that one sheep than about the ninety-nine that were never lost" (Matthew 18:12-13, NCV).*

Who do you love most fiercely, most protectively, most desperately here on earth? What would you do for them? Know that it's a mere fraction, nearly immeasurable, of what God would do for you. Spend some time thanking him for his great love.

PROCRASTINATION

I don't want to walk in late; I think I'll just go tomorrow.

I'm feeling a little tired; I probably wouldn't do my best today, anyway.

I don't feel very creative right now. I'll do it in the morning.

How often are circumstances ideal? How often do we think we need to wait until they are?

Right now, today, let's choose together to follow the advice of Scripture and decide that a few minutes late is better than absent. Let's acknowledge our collective fatigue, and then do today's version of our best in spite of it. Let's stop waiting for a burst of creativity, attack our projects, and see what happens. Let's honor God—and surprise ourselves at the same time.

Those who wait for perfect weather
will never plant seeds;
those who look at every cloud
will never harvest crops (Ecclesiastes 11:4, NCV).

What are you waiting for?

JANUARY 6

COMPASSION

Advertisers know your secret. They know the sight of a lost puppy, starving child, or grieving mother tugs at something deep inside your female heart, giving you a powerful desire to do something—anything. They're counting on it.

When we accepted Christ, and he gave us his Holy Spirit, we became aware of his heart. Specifically, we became aware of what breaks his heart. The more in tune we are with him, the more those things break our own hearts.

Jesus was pretty clear: "Feed my sheep," he commanded. His actions said the same; he fed them by the thousands. He wept for Lazarus' sisters in their grief. He wept for those who did not recognize him. He wept for us. He took on our burden of sin, the full weight of it, so we might live and know his heart.

Share each other's burdens, and in this way obey the law of Christ (Galatians 6:2, NLT).

What breaks your heart? Do you find yourself aching at the sight of a motherless child, a homeless mother, a neglected animal? How can you act on this compassion, and obey Christ?

JANUARY 7

GROWTH

Do you remember when you realized you had stopped growing? Your height was going to be your height, your shoe size your shoe size. This second fact was pretty thrilling for many of us; no more hearing Mom say, "That's too much to spend on shoes you'll outgrow in a few months." And so the collection began.

Not too long after our bones finish growing, we realize the real growth is just getting started. As we become young women, friendships either deepen or fade away as we begin to figure out who we are. No matter what our ages today, most of us are still working on that one. When we are growing in Christ, it's a process that never really ends.

> *I do not mean that I am already as God wants me to be. I have not yet reached that goal, but I continue trying to reach it and to make it mine. Christ wants me to do that, which is the reason he made me his (Philippians 3:12, NCV).*

How does knowing that God wants to help you become your best inspire you to attempt it this year?

THE BUDDY SYSTEM

Women like to travel in pairs. Men love to razz us for it, but it really does feel better to go to the restroom—or the concession stand, or the mall, or the movies, or to a child's basketball game—with another woman. It's not that it's uncomfortable being alone; it's just that most things are *better* with a companion. We go with our friends when they ask because we *want* to go.

How great it is to realize we have a constant companion in the Holy Spirit? Once we've accepted Jesus' free gift of salvation, we'll never be alone again. He's there for all of it—the silly, the simple, and the scary. Waiting for those test results, driving a lonely road at night, or walking an unfamiliar neighborhood by day, we are not alone. He is with us wherever we go. And like a true friend, he's there because he wants to be.

> *"This is my command—be strong and courageous! Do not be afraid or discouraged. For the Lord your God is with you wherever you go" (Joshua 1:9,* NLT*).*

Spend some quiet time feeling the ever-present Spirit of God. Thank him for his companionship.

JANUARY 9

NO WORDS

Sometimes, all you need to do to be a hero is show up. We love to talk, don't we? Words of encouragement, words of comfort, words of advice. Even if you are the quiet type, you know a woman who is rarely at a loss for words.

But occasionally, there really are no words. Someone you love is hurting, and you truly don't know what to say. Your presence says it all. Know that, in those moments you feel lost for words, if God occupies the central place in your heart, he'll make your heart known.

> *Then they sat on the ground with him for seven days and nights. No one said a word to Job, for they saw that his suffering was too great for words (Job 2:13, NLT).*

How easy or difficult would it be for you to simply be with someone in their sorrow and not try to "fix" them? Do you know someone who would be blessed today by the silent, loving presence of someone who loves them?

FOLLOW THE ARROW

Decisions, decisions. It seems a week never goes by without our needing to make at least one important choice. Whether job related, relationship motivated, or something as seemingly innocent as how to spend a free Friday, wouldn't it be nice to have an arrow pointing us in the right direction—especially if we are in danger of making a wrong turn?

According to the Word, we have exactly that. When we truly desire to walk the path God sets us on, and when we earnestly seek his voice, he promises to lead us in the right direction. His ever-present Spirit is right there, ready to put us back on the path each time we wander off.

Your ears shall hear a word behind you, saying,
"This is the way, walk in it,"
Whenever you turn to the right hand
or whenever you turn to the left" (Isaiah 30:21, NKJV*).*

Consider the decisions before you right now. To whom are you turning for guidance? Lay your options before God, and then listen for his voice.

JANUARY 11

THE JOY OF CERTAINTY

Yesterday we read about hearing God's voice behind us, leading us down the path he's chosen for our lives. Perhaps this idea isn't entirely comforting to you. *What about free will? What if I* want *to wander off the path a little bit?* The idea of just blindly following someone, even God himself, can seem a little daunting. What if his path is no fun?

Rest assured. You are not blindfolded, and he is not pushing you down his—or any—path. You will only hear his voice if you are listening, and the choice to follow his lead is entirely yours. But what a wonderful choice it is! Consider Psalm 16.

> *You will show me the path of life;*
> *in Your presence is fullness of joy;*
> *at Your right hand are pleasures forevermore (Psalm 16:11, NKJV).*

He doesn't just tell us which way to go, he *shows* us the path. And even better, because he is with us, joy and pleasure are ours—forever. Rest in that lovely assurance today, and pray for the courage to surrender to his lead.

YOU ARE PERFECT

Stop, go back, and read that again. You are perfect. Looking in the mirror, or thinking back over your day, it is easy to forget or disbelieve those words. Don't let that happen. A wrinkle here, a bulge there, an unkind word, or a jealous thought cannot change the way the Father sees you. And it's how he wants you to see yourself.

The dictionary uses 258 words to explain what it means to be perfect, but we only need to know this: We are *complete*. When he chose to die on the cross for our sins, Jesus took away every flaw from those of us who love him. He finished what we never could; he made us perfect.

By a single offering he has perfected for all time those who are being sanctified (Hebrews 10:14, ESV*).*

If possible, go to the mirror you see yourself in most often. Stand before it and ask God to show you what he sees when he looks at you. See past the flaws, past any hurt or anger in your eyes, past any perceived imperfection. See yourself complete, just as you were meant to be. See yourself perfect.

CONFIDENT IN OUR INCOMPETENCE

Whether bringing a brand new baby home from the hospital, giving your first major presentation at work, or simply making your first Thanksgiving meal, there's probably been at least one moment in your life that had you thinking, *I have no idea what I'm doing. I'm not qualified.* So what did you do? Chances are, you put a smile on your face, dove in, and did your best.

The older we get, the more we realize how truly helpless we are. We also, beautifully, realize it's okay. There is great freedom in admitting our shortcomings and allowing the Father to be our strength. No matter what he asks of us, we are confident in our incompetence. We may not be capable, but God is more than qualified to carry out his plans through us. All we need to do is swallow our pride and let him lead us.

> *It is not that we think we are qualified to do anything on our own. Our qualification comes from God (2 Corinthians 3:5, NLT).*

What dream or calling would you be able to fulfill if you were to embrace God's competence as your own?

JANUARY 14

CHOOSING WELL

How different would life be if you decided, today, to be done with your job? Whether CEO, barista, or dance instructor, your choice would be noticed. Lives would change. What would happen if you simply chose not to get out of bed tomorrow? Even a change of hair color has the potential to affect our trajectory. Our decisions matter—and not just here on earth.

God is interested in the choices you make. He has plans for you and desires for your life, but you have the final say. You get to choose. When it comes to the big stuff, all of heaven is waiting for your decision.

> *"So fear the LORD and serve him wholeheartedly. Put away forever the idols your ancestors worshiped when they lived beyond the Euphrates River and in Egypt. Serve the LORD alone. But if you refuse to serve the LORD, then choose today whom you will serve...But as for me and my family, we will serve the LORD" (Joshua 24:14-15, NLT).*

While the angels are probably not sitting around debating which shade of red you should try at your next salon visit, know that heaven is truly interested in how you choose to conduct your life. God waits for you to choose life—to choose him—every day.

JANUARY 15

WALK STEADY

What is it about high heels? Every family album contains a photo of an adorable toddler attempting to walk in Mama's shoes, and every woman remembers her first wobbly attempt to appear graceful in that first pair of pumps. How did she make it look so easy, so elegant? Most of us also have a memory of a not-so-graceful stumble or even a twisted ankle; yet, somehow the stiletto retains its appeal. Who hasn't relied on the steady arm of an escort or companion in far more sensible footwear?

Walking with Jesus is a little like learning to walk in four-inch heels. Others make it look so easy, gliding along apparently sinless while we feel shaky and uncertain, prone to stumble at any moment. Will we take a wrong step? Fall flat on our faces? (Do anyone else's feet hurt?) Lean on the strong arm of the Savior; allow him to steady you and direct your steps.

Direct my footsteps according to your word;
let no sin rule over me (Psalm 119:133, NIV*).*

In which aspect of your walk do you feel the most steady and certain? The least? Share your confidence and your concerns with the Savior, and invite him to lead you in both.

YOU ARE CHERISHED

It's good to be loved, isn't it? What feeling really compares to knowing someone has run through the rain, cancelled an international flight, driven all night—for you? Even if we've never experienced it, we've imagined it in our hearts. Or else we've had the realization that we, too, would move heaven and earth for the one we love the most. Whether husband, child, parent, sibling, or dear friend, to love and be loved deeply just may be the best feeling there is.

How much love you have given or received is a mere sampling of the way Jesus feels about you. You are cherished, loved beyond reason or measure. The one who really *can* move heaven and earth would do so in a heartbeat—for you.

> *I am convinced that neither death nor life, neither angels nor demons, neither the present nor the future, nor any powers, neither height nor depth, nor anything else in all creation, will be able to separate us from the love of God that is in Christ Jesus our Lord (Romans 8:38-39, NIV).*

Let the incredible words above wash over you as you realize there is nothing—absolutely nothing—Jesus wouldn't do for you.

JANUARY 17

WHEN YOUR HEART IS TROUBLED

I can't get a moment's peace. Sound familiar? We all go through seasons where it seems every corner hides a new challenge to our serenity, assuming we've actually achieved any semblance of serenity in the first place. Why is it so hard to find peace in this world? Because we're looking *in this world.*

After his resurrection, before Jesus ascended into heaven, he left his disciples with something they'd never had before: peace. More specifically, he gave them *his* peace, a gift not of this world. Whatever the world can offer us can also be taken from us. Any security, happiness, or temporary reprieve from suffering is just that: temporary. Only the things of heaven are permanent and cannot be taken away.

> *"Peace I leave with you; my peace I give you. I do not give to you as the world gives. Do not let your hearts be troubled and do not be afraid" (John 14:27,* NIV*).*

Do not *let* your heart be troubled, Jesus tells us. This means we have a choice. Share the things with him that threaten your peace, and then remember they have no hold on you. You are his, and his peace is yours.

HEARING GOD

The best way to know if something is true, or right, is to hear it for yourself—straight from the source. You believe you nailed the interview, but you don't believe you got the job until you get the phone call. You feel you might be pregnant, but you wait for the test results before telling anyone. The same is true for bad news, at least ideally. You get wind of a rumor about a friend's indiscretion, but you wait for her side of the story before believing a word.

So what about God? How can we hear from him? How do we discern his will for our lives? We may not have a hotline, but we do have his book. God speaks to us through his Word, so if you are waiting for confirmation, direction, validation, or conviction, pick it up. Read, and listen.

So faith comes from hearing, and hearing through the word of Christ (Romans 10:17, ESV).

How often do you feel God speaking to you through his Word? Are your conversations as frequent and meaningful as you'd like? Share you heart with him right now, and listen for his reply.

JANUARY 19

HE IS FAITHFUL

What's the oldest thing you own? How long have you had it, and what does it mean to you? Whether a decades-old diamond ring, twenty-year-old car, or a tattered baby blanket hanging together by threads, you probably know it won't last forever. How about your longest relationship? How many years have you been connected to this person through the good and the bad? One way we decide where to place our faith is longevity. History matters.

Consider now what God made: the earth we live on. Scientists estimate it to be 4.5 billion years old, give or take fifty million. Whether we think it's been around that long or six to ten thousand years, it's some quality workmanship. If we're looking for someone to trust, we won't find better credentials than that.

> *Your faithfulness flows from one generation to the next;*
> *all that you have created sits firmly in place to testify of you*
> *(Psalm 119:90, TPT).*

Through every storm, every disaster, every war, and every attack of the enemy, our earth stands. Ponder all God has made and all he has done, and share your heart with him regarding his faithfulness. Have you embraced it?

REMAIN FAITHFUL

A video of a small, white dog entering a hospital through the automatic doors and wandering its halls made national news recently. A short investigation revealed the dog's owner had been taken to the hospital earlier for cancer treatment. The dog bolted from the yard earlier that day and ran all the way—nearly two miles—to the hospital to see her owner. No one is sure how she knew where to go. She was led by love.

God desires that kind of faithfulness from us. He wants his daughters to seek him, to love him, with all of our hearts. May nothing stop us from returning his faithfulness with our own! Even—or perhaps especially—if we don't know where we are going, let us be led by love to show our faithfulness to our Father.

Hold on to loyal love and don't let go,
and be faithful to all that you've been taught.
Let your life be shaped by integrity,
with truth written upon your heart (Proverbs 3:3, TPT*).*

Do you see how much your Abba loves you? He desires your faithfulness so much he wants you to write it on your heart. What would it take for you to seek him that way, to bolt from the safety of your surroundings in search of him?

OWNING OUR SINS

Think of a time you blatantly denied something you had done. Maybe as a little girl, melted chocolate covering your face and hands, you swore you hadn't had any cookies. Perhaps more recently you lied to a girlfriend about betraying a confidence, or to your husband about the cost of a pair of jeans.

First off, don't beat yourself up. We are human, and it's hard to accept, and even harder to admit, when we've disappointed someone. As long as we've admitted our mistake, we are free to move on. Let's not miss that first part: we must *admit* it. Why? It's the reason Jesus died for us.

> *If we claim to be without sin, we deceive ourselves and the truth is not in us. If we confess our sins, he is faithful and just and will forgive us our sins and purify us from all unrighteousness. If we claim we have not sinned, we make him out to be a liar and his word is not in us (1 John 1:8-10, NIV).*

We are sinners. This fact is the whole reason for Jesus' life and death. Ask him to show you any sin you are denying or are unaware of, so you can confess it—and be set free.

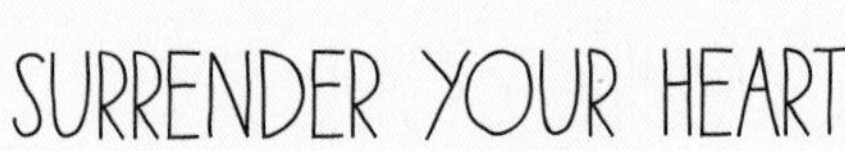

JANUARY 22

SURRENDER YOUR HEART

Watching the news we learn the losing army in a war has surrendered to their enemy. The fugitive has finally surrendered to police after a long standoff. Perhaps, closer to home, someone you know has surrendered to addiction. So how, given all these examples, are we supposed to feel good about surrendering to God? As women, it can feel particularly scary to allow ourselves to be vulnerable. Doesn't *surrender* mean defeat, giving up?

It would…if God were our enemy. But because he is for us and not against us, surrender means something else altogether. It means *freedom*. Surrender also means abandoning ourselves to God and no longer resisting him—accepting his plans and his perfect will for our lives. We don't have to strive any more once we give him our hearts.

O my son, give me your heart.
May your eyes take delight in following my ways
(Proverbs 23:26, NLT*).*

Is there an area of your heart you are struggling to hold onto? Consider that his plans are perfect, that his will for you is peace. What would it take for you to surrender your whole heart to him, and end the struggle?

REAL HUNGER

When was the last time you exclaimed, "I'm starving!"? How about, "I'm so full!"? Many of us say both things in a week. Occasionally at the beginning and end of a single meal. Clearly when we examine these terms literally, and in the greater context of a hungry world, we are not starving if we have the means to become full only minutes later. Chances are we don't even begin to know what that kind of hunger feels like. So what *are* we saying?

We are recognizing, by the empty, gnawing feeling in our bellies, an unmet need. Fortunately for most of the sisters reading these words, those physical needs can be easily taken care of. Why does the emptiness so often remain though? Because this is not our home. Jesus is our home, and until he returns, our hunger—in one way or another—will remain.

Poor people will eat until they are full;
those who look to the Lord will praise him.
May your hearts live forever! (Psalm 22:26, NCV*)*

The next time you feel hunger, whether physical or emotional, turn to Jesus and thank him for the reminder that he is the only thing that truly satisfies.

HOPE

What differentiates hope from a wish? Think about the lottery. Does one hope to win, or wish to win? How about a promotion, a pregnancy, or a proposal? Both hoping and wishing contain desire, but for wishing, that is where it ends. Hope goes deeper. The strong desire for something good to happen is coupled with a reason to believe that it will.

We see then how vital hope is, and why it's such a beautiful gift. Desire without hope is empty, but together they bring joy, expectancy, and peace. When we put our hope in Christ, he becomes our reason to believe good things will happen. He *is* our hope.

> *May the God of hope fill you with all joy and peace as you trust in him, so that you may overflow with hope by the power of the Holy Spirit (Romans 15:13,* NIV*).*

Allow this blessing from Romans to wash over you today as the Holy Spirit fills you with hope, joy, and peace. Believe good things will happen—you have a wonderful reason to.

JANUARY 25

THE REAL THING

Is that real? Whether body part, hair color, purse, or jewel, there's real, and there's imitation. Neither choice is inherently wrong or right. Why we choose as we do—and where we compromise—reveals our hearts. And it's our hearts that matter to God.

Make no mistake, a sister who shuns makeup and hasn't painted her house trim in years can be every bit as guilty of vanity and pride as one who won't leave her own bedroom until she appears flawless and has an eight-person grounds crew.

> *When they arrived, Samuel took one look at Eliab and thought, "Surely this is the Lord's anointed!"*
> *But the Lord said to Samuel, "Don't judge by his appearance or height, for I have rejected him. The Lord doesn't see things the way you see them. People judge by outward appearance, but the Lord looks at the heart" (1 Samuel 16:6-7, NLT).*

God doesn't care how much you spend on shoes, how much time you spend in front of the mirror, or how fabulous your home is. He does care about why those things matter—or don't—to you. Spend some time examining your heart with him today.

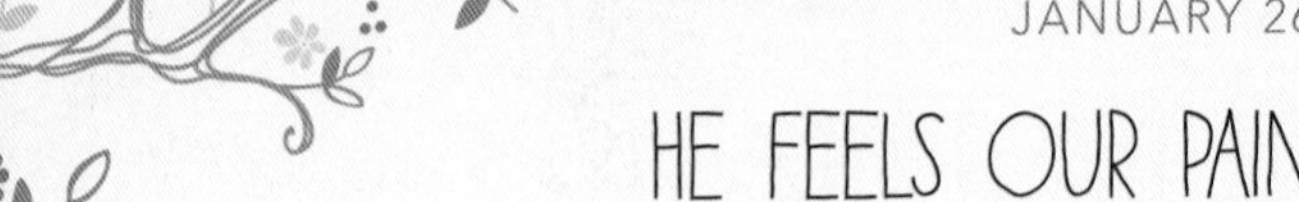

HE FEELS OUR PAIN

When someone we love is in pain, their ache becomes our ache. We cry openly with our newly jobless neighbors, recently bereaved girlfriends, freshly disappointed daughters. Tears come easy when your heart is surrendered to the Holy Spirit, because they are *his* tears. He hurts when we hurt.

In the shortest verse in the Bible, but also among the most beautiful, Jesus saw how his dear friends were hurting and was moved to tears. He knew he was about to take their pain away by raising Lazarus to life again, but in that moment, their pain was his pain—and it broke his heart.

Jesus wept (John 11:35, NASB).

In telling the story of Lazarus' death and resurrection (see John 11:1-46), why do you think these two words are set apart and given their own verse? How are you affected by them? Are you able to imagine Jesus openly weeping with Mary and Martha? Spend some time with your thoughts, and share with him your response to his great compassion.

REJOICE TODAY

Winter is fully upon us, and even if you live somewhere that isn't blanketed in cold and snow, it's still winter. It's not as warm outside, and there's not as much life in nature. If you *do* live where winter is cold, you may be growing tired of boots, hats, scarves (well, maybe not scarves), and puffy, shapeless coats. Looking outside, there may not be much to feel particularly joyful about.

Yet, we are called to rejoice—today. There are days we see his handiwork everywhere we look, and there are days that just seem to happen. Be certain; the Creator has created, and this day is it. Today is an offering from our Abba, our papa, to us. That in itself is cause for celebration, don't you think?

This is the day the Lord has made;
We will rejoice and be glad in it (Psalm 118:24, NKJV*).*

Let's look harder, closer, at today. Find a patch of blue sky, recall a night of sledding, light a fire. Turn your heart toward him, and rejoice and be glad for today.

NOTHING TO FEAR

A loud crash in the night. Unexpected footsteps falling uncomfortably close in a dark parking lot. A ringing phone at 3:00 AM. No matter how brave we think we are, certain situations quicken the pulse. We've heard, over and over, that we have nothing to fear if we walk with God, but let's be honest: certain situations are scary! So what does it mean to have nothing to fear?

Let's consider David's words from Psalm 56. When we are afraid, and we will be, we can give our situation to God and let him take the fear away. Notice it doesn't say he changes the situation, but that he changes our response to it. We have nothing to fear not because scary things don't exist, but because God erases our worry and replaces it with trust.

> *In the day that I'm afraid, I lay all my fears before you*
> *and trust in you with all my heart.*
> *What harm could a man bring to me?*
> *With God on my side I will not be afraid of what comes*
> *(Psalm 56:3-4, TPT).*

What are you afraid of? Have you truly tried letting go of that fear? If not, why? Talk to God about this.

FORGIVENESS

It seems like most families and many circles of friends contain at least two people who aren't speaking to one another—and haven't for years. Perhaps you know someone. Perhaps you *are* someone in this situation. Occasionally, the offense itself is truly unforgivable: abuse, betrayal, or complete disregard. Other times, and considerably more often, even the people involved admit the silliness of the quarrel and are no longer angry about it. But they're still angry with the person.

What do we gain when we hold onto bitterness? Bitterness. When we refuse to let go of anger, what do we find in our clenched fists? Anger. While an offense may be unforgivable, no person is. Jesus proved that when he died for *all of us*. And here's a fact often overlooked, especially by those of us who seem to like our little balls of anger: God withholds *our* forgiveness until we have forgiven others. Ouch.

> *"When you stand praying, if you hold anything against anyone, forgive them, so that your Father in heaven may forgive you your sins" (Mark 11:25,* NIV*).*

Sisters, let us encourage one another, and ourselves, to believe what Scripture tells us. Together, let's open our hands and surrender our grudges, and ask the Father to refill us with peace.

GRACE UPON GRACE

You know those days, the perfect ones? Your hair looks great, you nail a work assignment (whether client presentation, spreadsheet, or getting twins to nap at the same time), you say just the right thing and make someone's day, and then come home to find dinner waiting for you. It's good upon good, blessing upon blessing.

Being a daughter of the Almighty gains us access to that blessed feeling every day, even when our circumstances are ordinary or even difficult. His love is so full, and his grace so boundless, that when his Spirit lives in us even a flat tire can feel like a blessing. Our status as beloved daughters of the King guarantees it, we need only claim it.

For of His fullness we have all received, and grace upon grace (John 1:16, NASB*).*

Do you see God's grace poured out upon you today? Thank him for it.

JANUARY 31

HONOR IN PURITY

What do you think of when you hear the word *purity*? Perhaps a nun in her convent—someone who keeps herself completely untouched by the temptations of the world—an innocent child, or a great religious figure?

Often when we think about purity we think of a lack of obvious, outward sin. But both purity and impurity are birthed in the heart and developed in the mind long before they become expressed in action. Our purity is measured, not in what we do or what we have done, but in the hidden places of our heart's attitudes and our mind's wanderings.

> *So the Lord has rewarded me according to my righteousness,*
> *according to the cleanness of my hands in his sight*
> *(Psalm 18:24, ESV).*

If you ever wonder if your purity counts for anything—if refraining from the pleasures of sin is even worth it—be encouraged today. God will reward you according to your righteousness. He sees the intentions of your heart and the thoughts in your mind. He knows how badly you want to please him with your life, and he will bless you for it. He is honored in your purity, and that honor is the most important reward of all.

You shall go out in joy and be led forth in peace; the mountains and the hills before you shall break forth into singing, and all the trees of the field shall clap their hands.

Isaiah 55:12 ESV

FEBRUARY 1

THE PATIENCE PIT

Let's be honest, we're not that good at waiting for anything these days. Yet, the reality is that waiting is a necessary part of life. We wait for people, we wait for events, and we wait for desires to be fulfilled. But do we recognize that waiting might also apply to our emotional lives? Do we hold on to hope that we can be rescued from a troubled heart?

King David described himself as being in a pit of miry clay, likely another of his despairing moments, perhaps even on reflection of his sins. He needed to be rescued, not necessarily from his enemies, but from his state of mind. David says he *waited patiently,* understanding that he might not be instantly rescued. And he trusted that God alone would save him.

I waited and waited and waited some more;
patiently, knowing God would come through for me.
Then, at last, he bent down and listened to my cry
(Psalm 40:1, TPT).

Do you feel as though your emotions are on slippery ground or that your thoughts are stuck in the miry clay? Are you willing to wait patiently for the great rescuer to lift you up and place your feet on solid ground? Take a moment today to ask God for his help, recognize the necessity of waiting, and trust him for the rescue.

WORDS OF LIFE

It doesn't take long to realize the power of the tongue. As women, it can be our strongest device. There is no doubt that we are good at talking; the question is, do we talk *good*?

The words we allow to come out of our mouths can have great consequence. Once they are spoken, we cannot take them back. It is not only the words that we choose to say, sometimes it is the fact that we say them at all. As the Scripture says, even a small spark can set a great forest on fire!

> *When we put bits into the mouths of horses to make them obey us, we can turn the whole animal. Or take ships as an example. Although they are so large and are driven by strong winds, they are steered by a very small rudder wherever the pilot wants to go. Likewise, the tongue is a small part of the body, but it makes great boasts. Consider what a great forest is set on fire by a small spark (James 3:3-5, NIV).*

Ask God to forgive you for the times when you have sparked a fire. Allow the Holy Spirit to guide your heart and your thoughts so the words you speak are truthful, encouraging, and life-giving.

MATURE INNOCENCE

Kids are cute—except when they are throwing a tantrum in public, fighting with their siblings, or making silly gestures to the people in the car beside them. Of course, we don't expect children to act appropriately in all situations; they are still growing and learning. It would, however, seem absurd if we saw an adult sit down on the floor of the supermarket in protest, or wailing loudly that they didn't want to go home! We expect adults to think and act with maturity as they have developed their understanding and respect for others, along with virtues such as self-control.

Paul's expectation of the church in Corinth was that they would handle difficult situations, especially relationships with other Christians, with maturity. But there is an exception: Paul hoped that the church would be as innocent as infants in matters of evil. We should be very careful to stay away from evil thoughts and actions, and ensure that we grow in the things of God.

Do not be children in your thinking; yet in evil be infants, but in your thinking be mature (1 Corinthians 14:20, NASB*).*

Can you think of a situation that you might come across today that you will need to approach with maturity? Be encouraged that you are growing each day in the understanding of God and his Word. Be confident as you apply this understanding to your life.

IN LIGHT OF RESURRECTION

When Job was going through relentless suffering, he had a lot of opportunities to contemplate death. His pain was unbearable, he did not understand God's purpose for his misery, and he had no firm understanding of why God didn't grant him death. He was, for a time, with little hope.

Job did not have the benefit of understanding humanity through Christ's resurrection. Christ showed us that death has been conquered and that life will be resurrected and restored. Job had seen a glimpse of this reality in nature. He knew that when trees were cut down they sprouted again; yet, he did not make the connection that nature exposes God's design for humanity.

"At least there is hope for a tree:
If it is cut down, it will sprout again,
and its new shoots will not fail.
Its roots may grow old in the ground
and its stump die in the soil,
yet at the scent of water it will bud
and put forth shoots like a plant.
But a man dies and is laid low;
he breathes his last and is no more" (Job 14: 7-10, NIV).

Read this scripture again with the understanding that we are like the tree. There is hope in the light of Christ's resurrection that though we suffer, we will sprout again. Can you walk in this hope today?

FEBRUARY 5

DEEPER ROOTS

Calla lilies are beautiful flowers with wide, spotted leaves, thick stems, and bold colors. Year after year, you can watch the stunning leaves appear, and anticipate the gorgeous flowers…and then be disappointed when nothing more happens. Perhaps the soil is the problem? Calla lilies can be very particular.

It's a great picture of Jesus' parable of the sower and the seeds. Some seeds fall on rocky soil, and while God's Word is received, it doesn't take firm root and quickly withers at the sign of hardship. The seeds that are established in good soil, where the roots can go deep, not only survive, they also bear fruit.

> *"The one on whom seed was sown on the good soil, this is the man who hears the word and understands it; who indeed bears fruit and brings forth, some a hundredfold, some sixty, and some thirty" (Matthew 13:23, NASB).*

Do you hope to see more depth in your relationship with Jesus? Do you want others to see God's beauty displayed through your life? Be encouraged to hear the words of Jesus and then allow those words to penetrate your heart deeply until you understand them. Plant yourself in fertile soil, and watch the beauty that emerges.

HEART AND SOUL

We know the greatest commandment is to love the Lord our God with all our heart, soul, mind, and strength. It can be easy to say that we love God, but how do we show it?

King Josiah was one of the greatest examples in the Old Testament of loving God with all of his being. While the temple was being restored, a priest found the book of the law hidden in the walls. When Josiah read the law, he was grieved and immediately sprang into action. He renewed the Lord's covenant in front of all of Israel. He tore down every false idol, shrine, and high place that was associated with other gods.

> *Neither before nor after Josiah was there a king like him who turned to the Lord as he did—with all his heart and with all his soul and with all his strength, in accordance with all the Law of Moses (2 Kings 23:25,* NIV*).*

Are we grieved when we read God's Word and realize that we are far from keeping his commandments? Are we willing to take a stand against the idols of our culture? God was pleased with Josiah because his heart was responsive and he humbled himself before the Lord. Take some time today to renew your commitment to God and show him your love through obedience to his Word.

FEBRUARY 7

THE SPIRIT IS WILLING

Lord, I know the right thing to do, but I just don't have the strength to do it. This thought has likely been on our minds more often than we want to admit. We don't like to acknowledge that sometimes we just don't have it in us to make the right choice.

Paul understood the internal conflict that we face in doing right. As new creations in Christ, we have in us the desire to do good; however, as part of a fallen world, we are inherently selfish. In which direction do we position ourselves? We can dwell on our desire to do right, or on our desire to please ourselves. The more we set our minds in the right direction, the easier it will become.

> *I know that nothing good dwells in me, that is, in my flesh; for the willing is present in me, but the doing of the good is not (Romans 7:18,* NASB*).*

Above all, remember that it is the enabling power of Christ that you must rely on to continue to make the right decisions; it is through his grace that you can overcome. You know the right thing to do, and by his grace you will do it.

FEBRUARY 8

CREATURES OF HABIT

Wake up. Make bed. Get dressed. Coffee. Not always in that order, but you can guarantee that many do those things every single morning. They might also bite their nails, anger easily, and stay up too late. Patterns are hard to break. We are, after all, creatures of habit, and unfortunately not all of those habits are good.

What do you do when you are confronted with a habit that is not positive? Do you recognize when you rely on something just because it makes you feel accepted, comforted, or in control? Sometimes we aren't even conscious of our habits until we try to give them up.

Scripture says that establishing the right pattern begins with the renewing of our minds. This means that we must first acknowledge the need for change, and then submit our way of thinking to resemble that of Christ.

> *Do not conform to the pattern of this world, but be transformed by the renewing of your mind. Then you will be able to test and approve what God's will is—his good, pleasing and perfect will (Romans 12:2,* NIV*).*

Can you trust God today to show you his good, pleasing, and perfect will as you submit your worldly habits to him?

FEBRUARY 9

ONE PERCENT WRONG

There's a story of a man who was arguing with his wife in their first year of marriage. The disagreement ended with one of them storming from the room. While the husband was praying for his wife to see that she was wrong, he felt the Holy Spirit's prompt: "How wrong are *you* in this?" Even though the man was convinced he was only one percent wrong, he was convicted to deal with that one percent, and leave the wife's ninety-nine percent to God.

It's pretty easy to find fault in other people. We are often blind to our own errors and weaknesses. It can be hard to uncover our sin, especially in situations where we feel certain we are right!

If you cover up your sin you'll never do well.
But if you confess your sins and forsake them,
you will be kissed by mercy.
Guard your life carefully and be tender to God,
and you will experience his blessings.
But the stubborn, unyielding heart will experience even greater evil (Proverbs 28:13-14, TPT*).*

Have you had an argument recently, and left convinced that the other person was the one in the wrong? Consider what percent wrong *you* were. Even if it is small, confess your wrongdoing, and be prepared to forgive the ninety-nine percent. Don't let your heart be hardened. Let his mercy toward you become your strength to forgive.

FEBRUARY 10

BODY PARTS

A tooth is such a small part of the body, but when it begins to ache, it can be debilitating! The human body is fascinating in this way. God has created all of our parts to be distinct yet interdependent.

As a Christian, you are part of the body of Christ. More important than trying to distinguish *which* part you are is the recognition of just how important your unique gifts are to the health of the whole body. You were created to belong to something that is greater than yourself.

> *Just as each of us has one body with many members, and these members do not all have the same function, so in Christ we, though many, form one body, and each member belongs to all the others. We have different gifts, according to the grace given to each of us (Romans 12:4-6,* NIV*).*

The Bible acknowledges that God has given us different gifts that are not for our individual gain. God designed our gifts to be used in harmony with others' gifts. Will you allow God to speak to you today about how you can use your gifts for the good of the entire body of Christ?

FEBRUARY 11

SLOW TO SPEAK

Do you ever feel like you are not being heard? It can be frustrating and discouraging when you realize the person you are talking to is not really listening.

For some, listening comes naturally; for others, it is something that has to be worked on. There is an art to listening. It begins with having the intention of being slow to speak. Take time to think through what others are saying to you. Try to understand where they are coming from. Discern if they just need to talk. Wait for them to ask your opinion and consider if your response will be helpful.

> *Take note of this: Everyone should be quick to listen, slow to speak and slow to become angry (James 1:19, NIV).*

Are you willing to tune in to what others are saying today? It may be a gentle rebuke, some great advice, or an encouraging word. Whatever it is, allow God's grace in your conversations, and humbly listen to what he wants you to hear.

MEDITATE ON GOODNESS

Do you ever catch yourself dwelling on the negative aspects of life? We can be nonchalant when someone tells us good news, but talk for hours about conflict, worries, and disappointment. It is good to communicate things that aren't going so well in our lives, but we can also fall into the trap of setting our minds on the wrong things.

Paul saw the need to address this within the church of Philippi. It seems there were people in the church that thought too highly of themselves and allowed discord to reside in their midst. Think of what dwelling on the negative actually does: it creates feelings of hopelessness, discouragement, and a lack of trust in our God who is good, true, and just.

> *Whatever is true, whatever is honorable, whatever is right, whatever is pure, whatever is lovely, whatever is of good repute, if there is any excellence and if anything worthy of praise, dwell on these things (Philippians 4:8, NASB).*

Do you need to ask for forgiveness for a heart that has been too negative? Can you find anything in your life and the lives of others that have virtue or are worthy of praise? Choose to dwell on the true, noble, just, pure, and lovely things, and experience the refreshing nature of a positive outlook.

FEBRUARY 13

TRUST WITH ALL OF YOUR HEART

Trust can be a hard word to put into action mostly because our experience with others tells us that we can be sorely disappointed. People let us down in many ways. We can even be disappointed in ourselves.

Remember the trust game that involved standing with eyes closed and falling back into the hands of a few peers in hopes that they would catch you? There was risk involved in that game, and it didn't always turn out well. Nothing can truly be guaranteed in this life, can it? Well, it depends on where you place your trust.

Trust in the Lord with all your heart,
And lean not on your own understanding;
In all your ways acknowledge Him,
And He shall direct your paths (Proverbs 3:5-6, NKJV*).*

God watches over us, cares for us, and is involved in our lives. When we acknowledge that every good thing comes from him, our faith is strengthened and we are able to trust him more. Make a point of noticing how God directs your paths today, and thank him for being trustworthy.

FEBRUARY 14

GOD IS LOVE

This "day of love" often carries many emotions—some positive, others not. It can be exciting for those falling in love, nostalgic for those who have been in love, disappointing for those who have not yet found love, and sorrowful for those that have lost love.

Take the romantic notion out of it, and love is still at the core of our beings. We recognize it through our relationships with family and friends. Love *is* to be celebrated! But let's be reminded of where love comes from. It's from God. And he alone is the only true example of it.

> *Beloved, let us love one another, for love is from God, and whoever loves has been born of God and knows God. Anyone who does not love does not know God, because God is love (1 John 4:7-8,* ESV*).*

Whatever love camp you are in today, remember that God is the one who is always faithful. He is the one that keeps his promises, and he will forever show his love to the world. What about *your* part? Are you able to show your love for God today?

FEBRUARY 15

A LOVE WITHOUT FEAR

God is an awesome God. He is all-powerful and he is holy. When we compare ourselves to such greatness, we can be overwhelmed with our insignificance. God is the author of life and death, and he determines our eternity!

But we know that God is love, and because of his love, he created a way for us to approach him boldly. He made us righteous and holy through the redemption of Christ. We are no longer in fear of punishment from a powerful God. Human love can involve fear because it is not perfect. It can disappoint, it can be taken away, and it can create a power imbalance that highlights our insecurities.

> *There is no fear in love. But perfect love drives out fear, because fear has to do with punishment. The one who fears is not made perfect in love (1 John 4:18,* NIV*).*

Do you compare God's love for you with the earthly love you have experienced? Acknowledge your struggle to accept God's perfect love. Allow yourself to love, and to be loved, without fear.

PERFECT IN OUR WEAKNESS

Have you ever taken a personality test to identify your strengths and weaknesses? You probably know if you are an introvert or extravert, whether you are creative or administrative, good at speaking, or great at listening. You probably also know all too well what your weaknesses are. You might be over-analytical, self-doubting, unorganized, or lacking empathy. There are areas in our life that we certainly don't feel proud of!

Paul, on the other hand, says he would rather boast about his weaknesses! Paul knew that his weaknesses made him rely on the power of the Holy Spirit.

> *"My grace is sufficient for you, for power is perfected in weakness." Most gladly, therefore, I will rather boast about my weaknesses, so that the power of Christ may dwell in me (2 Corinthians 12:9,* NASB*).*

You may be facing something that you are worried about because it is outside of your comfort zone. Will you consider that God can shine through you as you acknowledge your complete reliance on his Holy Spirit? It is not really the weakness in which you boast, but rather the power of Christ that is revealed through your weakness.

FEBRUARY 17

CREATION CLUES

It doesn't take much to marvel at creation. Looking up into the night sky, sitting on a shoreline, hiking through a forest, or watching a bud begin to blossom, our encounters with nature are many. But we don't often take the time to truly notice how incredible creation is.

God chose to reveal himself to us in a profound way. He knew that we would have appreciation for the beauty of nature that surrounds us. His invisible qualities are represented through something visible. And we describe it as beautiful, awesome, and perfect. This is God.

> *Since the creation of the world God's invisible qualities—his eternal power and divine nature—have been clearly seen, being understood from what has been made, so that people are without excuse (Romans 1:20, NIV).*

Take a look around at God's creation today and dwell on the quality of God that is represented. Allow yourself time to reflect on God's divinity and eternal power, and thank him for sharing it with you in a very real way.

REWARDS OF FELLOWSHIP

When was the last time you felt spiritually recharged from conversation or prayer with other Christians? Sometimes going to church, a woman's group, or a Bible study seems like just another thing to add to your list of things to do.

God is a relational God. He knows that we need each other, and that life is better together. As a Christian, it is especially important to share time with other believers. When we make time to pray together, study the Bible together, and share our faith stories, we can be supported, encouraged, and strengthened.

"Where two or there are gathered together in my name, I am there in the midst of them" (Matthew 18:20, NKJV).

Are you giving yourself an opportunity to be uplifted by other believers or to be an encouragement to those around you? Remember that God promises to be with you when you are gathered together in his name. Let's actively seek his presence together, and experience the rich rewards of fellowship.

FEBRUARY 19

WHEN BEING RICH IS HARD

If only I had more money! The thought runs through our minds frequently, and though we may actually have enough to be content with, we are often thinking about what we could do with more.

Wherever you stand financially, you probably have a goal of accumulating more wealth than you have now. But did you ever notice how the Bible seems to view earthly riches as actually getting in the way of our relationships with God and others?

> *"If you wish to be complete, go and sell your possessions and give to the poor, and you will have treasure in heaven; and come, follow Me." But when the young man heard this statement, he went away grieving; for he was one who owned much property (Matthew 19:21-22, NASB).*

Wealth is rarely what we hope it is; the more we have, the more we have to lose. Jesus wanted the rich man to have a compassionate heart—one that was willing to give up what he had for the sake of the kingdom. To do this, he would have needed to give up the life that he was accustomed to. Before asking God to bless you with wealth, ask him to bless you with a heart of giving.

STARS

If you have ever had the chance to be in a remote location on a clear night, you will know what it is like to look up into the sky and marvel at the magnificent display of stars. It is such a breathtaking view—one that reminds us of the greatness of our God.

Many times in the Bible, humanity is compared to the stars. We are reminded of how many people God has created. Yet, God says that he both leads and calls them by name. If the stars appear magnificent, then how much more magnificent is the one who created them? We worship a God that is able to remember each of us by name, and to know that not one of us is missing.

Lift up your eyes on high
And see who has created these stars,
The One who leads forth their host by number,
He calls them all by name;
Because of the greatness of His might
and the strength of His power,
Not one of them is missing (Isaiah 40:26, NASB*).*

Do you feel insignificant in God's great world today? Remember that God has a perfect plan for this world, and you complete this plan. Lift up your eyes and know that he knows your name, and that you are not missing from his plan.

FEBRUARY 21

BE CONTENT

She has great hair, looks energetic and fit, and has a doting husband and cute kids. She sings beautifully in church, is a great cook, and never says a bad word about anyone. She is smart and organized and holds a weekly Bible study at her house. She is everything we are not!

We spend a lot of our time comparing ourselves with others, and it can often lead to envy. God asks us to conduct ourselves in a way that is not envious, but content. When we compare ourselves to others, we choose to dwell on what we do not have rather than the good things that God has given us.

The Lord is all I need.
He takes care of me.
My share in life has been pleasant;
my part has been beautiful (Psalm 16:5-6, NCV).

God created us as we are, and he declared his creation to be good. Furthermore, he has given us the gift of always being near. To know that Jesus is right next to us, all the time, is really all we need. This is the contentment that Bible speaks of. Are you able to realize God's presence with you today, and let that fill you with contentment?

BETTER THAN RUBIES

If you were granted the one thing that you desire most, what would it be? We can probably answer this question better if we think of who or what we idolize. Whose life do we want, or what quality do we most admire? Beauty, intelligence, creativity, recognition, or love?

King Solomon understood the value of wisdom better than any other. When God offered him anything he desired, King Solomon responded with a request for wisdom. He could have asked for fame, or riches, or success in warfare; instead, he asked for *understanding*. King Solomon sought knowledge and instruction first, and ended up being the most wise, wealthy, famous, successful king that ever lived.

Receive my instruction, and not silver,
And knowledge rather than choice gold;
For wisdom is better than rubies,
And all the things one may desire cannot be compared with her (Proverbs 8:10-11, NKJV*).*

Silver, gold, and rubies are rare and precious elements. They are beautiful, strong, and valuable. Perhaps you own, or are even wearing, jewelry with precious metal and stone. Remind yourself of the greater value of wisdom, and be encouraged to seek Godly understanding above anything else.

FEBRUARY 23

BREAKTHROUGH

Are you waiting for a breakthrough in your circumstances? Maybe you have been praying for an unbelieving family member, a strained relationship, an answer to your financial stress, or clarity for a big decision ahead. Fasting doesn't often top the list of what to do when you really need that breakthrough, and it's not that hard to guess why it isn't a popular option. Eating is one of the most necessary and natural impulses—it takes a lot of self-control and personal effort to stop.

Consider what the Bible says about fasting, and notice how it goes hand in hand with prayer. There is a certain humility that accompanies fasting; it requires sobriety of heart, reflection, and focus. It brings your impulses into submission and gives you confidence in your self-control. More importantly, it seems to let the Lord know that you mean business—that you are ready to receive his revelation and guidance.

> *Then I set my face toward the Lord God to make request by prayer and supplications, with fasting, sackcloth, and ashes (Daniel 9:3,* NKJV*).*

Can you commit to make fasting a spiritual discipline in your life? You may just get the answers you were looking for, and perhaps even ones that you were not!

HEALING THROUGH JESUS

It is hard to understand how and when God heals his children. Have you prayed for healing recently and haven't got any better? Do you know someone around you that is unwell and not recovering? It can be disheartening when you are sick, or see others that you care about not improving.

Our faith does not need to be great, but through our belief in Jesus, we can also acknowledge our belief in the miracles that he performed. Jesus showed us that what we think is impossible is not impossible with God.

> *Jesus was going throughout all Galilee, teaching in their synagogues and proclaiming the gospel of the kingdom, and healing every kind of disease and every kind of sickness among the people (Matthew 4:23, NASB).*

Sometimes healing doesn't come, and we need to trust that God is still faithful and gracious. He will restore perfect health to us in eternity. We may have to wait for healing and we may never really know why. But let us still be encouraged today to believe in a God of miracles, and pray with all our might that he will bring healing to the sick.

ANGER MANAGEMENT

Have you ever been mad enough that you actually tremble? Sometimes we can get overwhelmed with emotions of anger—sometimes for good reasons, and sometimes not. Whatever the reason, the Bible speaks of the need to take some time out to calm down.

God is not overly concerned with the fact that we get angry. He understands the emotions of his creation. However, acting out in anger never achieves anything good. The Psalmist knew that sin often followed anger. Fortunately, we are given a helpful technique in how to handle our anger.

> *Be angry, and do not sin.*
> *Meditate within your heart on your bed, and be still*
> *(Psalm 4:4, NKJV).*

When you feel angry, go to your room or a quiet place. Be still, and listen to your heart. Allow God to calm your heart and speak to you in the quietness. The anger may still be present, but if you submit to the work of the Holy Spirit, you can keep yourself from sin.

ADORNMENT

Women like to look their best. This usually means wearing the right clothes, hairstyle, and accessories to match. Sometimes just getting our hair right can be the difference between a good or bad day! We need to admit our superficial nature and recognize when we are prioritizing outward appearance over inner beauty.

The Bible doesn't condemn outward adornment; rather, it is advises that we pay more attention to the "hidden person of the heart." Who is the woman on the inside? Are you doing your best to make that inner woman beautiful? Beauty, to God, is a gentle and quiet spirit.

> *Do not let your adornment be merely outward—arranging the hair, wearing gold, or putting on fine apparel—rather let it be the hidden person of the heart, with the incorruptible beauty of a gentle and quiet spirit, which is very precious in the sight of God (1 Peter 3:3-4, NKJV).*

Can you say that you act in gentleness towards others? Do you need to maintain a quiet spirit? Unlike outward beauty, these qualities get better with time. Learn to adorn yourself with true beauty, and deliberately display the hidden beauty that is precious to God.

FEBRUARY 27

PRUNED

Take a moment to reflect on a time when you felt you were giving the best of yourself. You may be thinking of times when you were utilizing your gifts and talents and could witness your positive influence in others around you. You may not have to reflect back that far, or you could be wondering where those times have gone!

Jesus describes himself as the vine. If we are being nourished from that source, we will produce fruit. In the times where we feel like we are not flourishing, it may be that the Father needs to do some necessary pruning—for the health of both the branch and the whole vine.

> *"I am the true vine, and my Father is the gardener. He cuts off every branch in me that bears no fruit, while every branch that does bear fruit he prunes so that it will be even more fruitful" (John 15:1-2, NIV).*

Rather than despair over his pruning, be encouraged that God has seen the fruit you have produced and is allowing a period of dormancy so that you will flourish once again. Take some time today to reflect on your gifts, submit them to Jesus, and wait expectantly for the great gardener to bring them back to life.

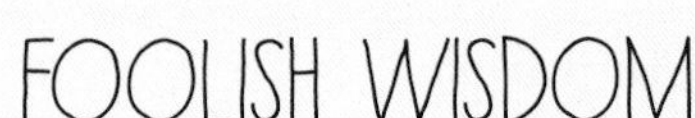

FOOLISH WISDOM

Our culture today is one that values intelligence and an educated mind; philosophers and the "great thinkers" are among the highly esteemed. It can be easy to get caught up (or left behind!) in debates of religion, politics, and philosophy. The problem with worldly wisdom is that it is self-generated; it exists in the context of a finite mind that cannot grasp the mysteries of God.

When Jesus came into the world, whom did he upset the most? That's right, the Scribes and the Pharisees—the most learned people of that time. He turned their ideas and assumptions upside-down and frustrated their intelligence! God's wisdom is for those who are humble enough to accept his ways. This is how he makes the foolish wise.

"I will destroy the wisdom of the wise;
the intelligence of the intelligent I will frustrate."
Where is the wise person? Where is the teacher of the law? Where is the philosopher of this age? Has not God made foolish the wisdom of the world? (1 Corinthians 1:19-20, NIV)

The next time you feel yourself unable to answer the intellectual bully, ask yourself what the source of their wisdom is. Trust in the wisdom of Jesus—it is eternal and life-giving.

MARCH

Therefore we do not lose heart, but though our outer man is decaying, yet our inner man is being renewed day by day. For momentary, light affliction is producing for us an eternal weight of glory far beyond all comparison.

2 Corinthians 4:16-17 NASB

CONSTANT LOVE

Have you ever been shown a kindness that you didn't deserve? What did it feel like to be given love when you deserved hate? To be given a second chance when all you should have gotten was a door slammed in your face?

We will wrong one another and we will be wronged by others. It's the human condition. But that is why the love of God is the only perfect solution for us. Love can cover even a million wrongs. When we choose love and kindness over anger and revenge, the sins that seemed so intense suddenly fade away. Love is the presence of Jesus in us, and Jesus is the only true anecdote for sin.

Above all, maintain constant love for one another, for love covers a multitude of sins (1 Peter 4:8, NRSV*).*

Constant love won't come naturally to you. Your humanity will cry out from within you and anger and rage will bubble forth without conscious invitation. But when you rely on the Spirit of God to intervene in your life and in your relationships, he can make kindness your response and love your reaction. Ask him to fill you with his Spirit and release his love in your heart so that you can walk fully in his presence.

MARCH 2

INTO THE LIGHT

All women seem to agree that fitting room mirrors are unpleasant. Something about that fluorescent lighting draws attention to all of our flaws. We would much rather admire our reflections in the flattering light of a glowing campfire or a few well-placed lamps. Bright light exposes every flaw. What was concealed in the darkness becomes glaringly obvious in the light.

God is very clear throughout Scripture that our sin makes us dead. When we are entrenched in sin, it is as though we are asleep. But when we bring our sin out from the darkness and into the light, Christ shines on us and frees us from our bondage of sin and death.

> *Do not participate in the unfruitful deeds of darkness, but instead even expose them; But all things become visible when they are exposed by the light, for everything that becomes visible is light. For this reason it says,*
> *"Awake, sleeper,*
> *And arise from the dead,*
> *And Christ will shine on you"* (Ephesians 5:11, 13-14, NASB).

The longer we hide our sin in low lighting and flatter ourselves in it, the longer we sleep and miss out on the good things that God has for us. Release whatever secret, hidden sin you are clinging to today and bask in his glorious light.

A THOUSAND GENERATIONS

How do you trust God when you feel betrayed by him? What strength is there for the moments when you feel as though the Creator of the universe has simply looked the other way? You know in your heart that he has control over every infinitesimal life, and yet he seems to have failed with yours. He promises peace, but your world is in turmoil. He offers joy, but pain is all you can feel. Dreams and purpose flooded your heart, and then were ripped from you.

Is God really faithful? Can he be trusted with our lives? With our hearts? Yes! He will keep his covenant to *a thousand* generations. That's roughly estimated as 20,000 years—a long time to remain faithful to someone. The same God that spoke to Moses and led the Israelites out of captivity in a whirlwind of miraculous power is covenanted to do the same for us.

> *Know therefore that the Lord your God is God, the faithful God who keeps covenant and steadfast love with those who love him and keep his commandments, to a thousand generations (Deuteronomy 7:9,* ESV*).*

The God who called Lazarus out of his grave, is with you in the same measure of power. The God who loved David through all his sin and brokenness loves you just as steadfastly. Rest in his covenant and trust that he will keep his Word.

MARCH 4

LET ME FIRST...

Obedience to Christ is both an awesome and challenging endeavor. Listening to the voice of God and obeying that voice isn't easy. God will ask us to do things that don't make sense, and his schedule will not always line up with our own.

It can be tempting for us to want our "ducks in a row" before we start following Christ into something. With our human agendas and preferences, we like to make sure we've crossed off our to-do lists before moving forward.

> *To another he said, "Follow me." But he said, "Lord, first let me go and bury my father." But Jesus said to him, "Let the dead bury their own dead; but as for you, go and proclaim the kingdom of God." Another said, "I will follow you, Lord; but let me first say farewell to those at my home." Jesus said to him, "No one who puts a hand to the plow and looks back is fit for the kingdom of God" (Luke 9:59-62,* NRSV*).*

When God speaks to you and calls you to something, instead of telling him what you need to do first, obey without hesitation. God isn't interested in the to-do lists of this world. He has a kingdom agenda with an eternal perspective. If you could see what he can see, you would never say, "Let me first..."

MARCH 5

STRESS

We are all well acquainted with stress. There are so many things in our life that cause us to be worried, pressured, and anxious. The world constantly presents us with unknowns and predicaments that steal our joy and rob our peace.

When we get in the presence of God and spend time in his Word, we are able to escape the stress of our lives and place our problems in his hands. God gives a peace that is unlike anything the world offers. He is focused on preparing us for his permanent kingdom, and, as a result, his presence offers hope and everlasting joy that is opposite to the trivial stressors of this life.

Those who love your instructions have great peace and do not stumble (Psalm 119:165, NLT*).*

Spend time in his presence today, letting his peace wash over your heart. Focus on his truth and his capability rather than your problems and incapacity. God is able to take everything that is troubling you today and exchange it for peace that is beyond what you can imagine.

MARCH 6

WISDOM OF SOLOMON

If you could ask for one thing from God, what do you think it would be? Money, happiness, love, success… any one of us would love to be given any of these things in full measure.

Solomon, a man who we know had an appetite for pleasure, took hold of his opportunity and asked for the best thing he possibly could have—wisdom. And God gave it to him. In all of life, don't we need wisdom the most? Wisdom to know what to do, how to act, and how to understand?

> *"You did not ask for a long life, or riches for yourself, or the death of your enemies. Since you asked for wisdom to make the right decisions, I will do what you asked" (1 Kings 3:11-12, NCV).*

We have the same privilege as Solomon: to ask God for wisdom, knowing that he will give it. What area of your life do you need wisdom for? Maybe you're on the edge of a huge decision, a choice that will affect your life forever. God says that what you need—wisdom—is yours for the taking. Ask God to come into the midst of whatever confusion you are faced with. Ask him to give you the same wisdom that he gave Solomon.

MARCH 7

COMPARISON

In the age of social media, comparison has become an easier default for us than it's ever been before. When every image we see of others has been properly angled, edited, filtered, and cropped we are quickly led into the delusion that the lives we see portrayed in those images are perfect. We believe that the smiling faces we see in that post are always smiling, and the perfect homes with the beautiful lighting are permanently well-kept and polished.

The danger of these filtered images is that we end up comparing ourselves to something that isn't an accurate standard. What we don't see is the life outside that frame. We don't see the mess, the struggles, and the imperfections that are inevitably part of every life—even the perfect-looking ones.

> *Let everyone be sure that he is doing his very best, for then he will have the personal satisfaction of work well done and won't need to compare himself with someone else (Galatians 6:4, TLB).*

God wants you to be so invested in the work that he has given you to do that you are not distracted or dissatisfied by what you see someone else doing. By diving headfirst into your unique life, you are saying yes to contentment and joy and moving forward into greater fulfillment and happiness.

MARCH 8

LOSS OF CONTROL

120: the last number she saw the needle pass on the speedometer. In one blinding instant, the wheels screeched, the glass broke, the pressure increased, the pain surged. All she could see was light and dark—flashes and fear. All she could hear was the deafening silence. And all she knew with certainty was that she had lost control.

Have you ever had a moment where you've felt completely out of control? A car accident, a diagnosis, or some other frightening moment? There are instances in our lives when our own flesh fails us. We recognize in a flash that we are no longer in control of our own outcome—and it terrifies us.

> *My flesh and my heart fail;*
> *But God is the strength of my heart and my portion forever (Psalm 73:26, NKJV).*

In that moment, when control is lost and fear overcomes, there is one thing we can know for certain. He is our strength; God never loses control. When your life, and the outcome of it, is ripped from your hands, it's still resting firmly in his grasp. He is our portion. He is our ration. He is enough. Release yourself today into the control of the only one who will never lose control.

CONSCIOUS CHOICE

Would you want someone to love you if they didn't really want to? If someone were forced or even paid to love you but you knew their love wasn't genuine, would you enjoy that type of love?

We have the conscious ability to choose whether or not we will love God. God will not make us love him or force us to follow him. The freedom that we have to choose is the most wonderful *and* the most fearful gift we have been given.

> *"Today I have given you the choice between life and death, between blessings and curses. Now I call on heaven and earth to witness the choice you make. Oh, that you would choose life, so that you and your descendants might live!" (Deuteronomy 30:19, NLT)*

You have a choice that no one can make for you. Life or death, it's up to you. God longs for you to choose life because he knows what wonderful things await those who respond to his love. He wants lovers who will worship him in spirit and in truth. He doesn't want false love, so he allows you to choose. What will you do with that choice today?

MARCH 10

PURSUIT OF PEACE

Women are emotionally driven. We are easily swayed by our feelings in many situations. And while there are many things that we women are strong in, our emotions are something we often feel we have little control over.

It can be easy to get emotionally entangled in arguments or tense situations. We are naturally curious, and we take great interest in what's going on in others' lives. Oftentimes our curiosity is driven by an honest fascination with people and relationships, but if we are not careful, we can easily cross the fine line into gossip and—for lack of a better term—drama.

Keep turning your back on every sin,
and make "peace" your life motto.
Practice being at peace with everyone (Psalm 34:14, TPT*).*

We are not only to look for peace, we are to chase after it. When someone comes to you and shares a concerning tidbit about a mutual friend, does judging that person create peace in her life or yours? Or does it only add to an already turbulent situation, and cause you stress in an area where none belonged to you? To pursue peace, we must turn from the desire to gossip, judge, and slander, and instead be kind, loving, and gentle.

VULNERABILITY

Some of the most substantial and ultimately wonderful changes in our lives come from moments of vulnerability: laying our cards on the table, so to speak, and letting someone else know how much they really mean to us. But vulnerability takes one key ingredient: humility. And humility is not an easy pill to swallow.

Isn't it sometimes easier for us to pretend that conflict never happened than to face the fact that we made a mistake and wronged another person? It's not always easy to humble ourselves and fight for the resolution in an argument—especially when it means admitting our failures.

He gives us more grace. That is why Scripture says:
"God opposes the proud
but shows favor to the humble" (James 4:6, NIV).

Who are you in the face of conflict? Do you avoid apologizing in an attempt to save face? Does your pride get in the way of vulnerability, or are you willing and ready to humble yourself for restoration in your relationships? God says that he will give favor and wisdom to the humble. What can you do today to humble yourself for the sake of a restored relationship?

MARCH 12

THE POWER OF BELIEF

Many times when we come into the presence of God, we become acutely aware of our inadequacies. Just as Adam and Eve did after they sinned, we recognize our own nakedness and the reality that before an all-knowing God, we can hide nothing.

We worry about the things in our lives that we are scared won't add up. We worry that we aren't quite enough: not gentle enough, faithful enough, or good enough. We want to please God with our lives, but we can easily get caught in a discouraging downward spiral when we focus on our own flaws.

> *What does the Scripture say? "Abraham believed God, and it was counted to him as righteousness" (Romans 4:3,* ESV*).*

God isn't asking for perfection. He knew we could never achieve that—which is precisely why he sent Jesus. What God wants from us is simply our belief. Believing God credits us with righteousness—something we can never attain in and of ourselves. Instead of focusing on your shortcomings when you stand in God's presence, believe what he says about you. Your belief will not go without credit.

MARCH 13

IMPOSSIBLE

What seems impossible to you today? What have you given up on, walked away from, and written off as absurd? What dreams have you let die simply because you felt they were unattainable?

Maybe our dreams, though they seem far off, were placed in our hearts for a purpose. And maybe they won't look exactly the way we always thought they would, but maybe they'll still come true in a new way. Maybe the things that seem insurmountable to us will be easily overcome when we simply shift perspective and look at them differently.

Behold, I will do a new thing,
Now it shall spring forth;
Shall you not know it?
I will even make a road in the wilderness
And rivers in the desert (Isaiah 43:19, NKJV*).*

Beloved, you serve a God who is powerful enough to make a path appear right through an empty wilderness and create a stream of life-giving water in the midst of a desert. He is more than able to take even the most impossible of situations and provide clarity, direction, and the means to make it through. Trust him with your impossibilities and rely on his strength for your weaknesses.

MARCH 14

SHARPENING

As Christians, we are meant to hold one another accountable to live a life worthy of our calling. But as nice as that sounds, it can be difficult to feel qualified to confront a fellow Christian who is walking in sin.

Godly confrontation isn't necessarily easy, but it *is* our responsibility. We must take a no-compromise stance when it comes to the health of the body of Christ. Before you confront another Christian who is in sin though, ask yourself if you are living by the Spirit. Are you listening to the Spirit's leading rather than your own selfish motives?

As iron sharpens iron,
so a friend sharpens a friend (Proverbs 27:17, NLT).

In order to bring sharpening, speak in gentleness and with grace—remembering the mercy that you have been shown by God. Encourage your brother or sister to repent and return, and offer to walk alongside them as they pursue righteousness and restoration.

COME CLOSE

Do you ever feel like you can't feel God? Like you've lost sight of him somehow? Sometimes we aren't sure how to get back to that place where we feel his presence strongly and hear his voice clearly.

We go through seasons where we feel distant from God, but the beautiful truth is that he has never gone anywhere. He's in the same place he was the first time we met him. God is unchanging and unwavering. His heart is always to be with us, and he never turns his back on his children.

> *Come close to God, and God will come close to you. Wash your hands, you sinners; purify your hearts, for your loyalty is divided between God and the world (James 4:8,* NLT*).*

God will not push himself on you. He will not share his glory with another, and he will not try to compete with the world for your heart. But, beloved, if you draw near to him, he will wrap you in the sweetness and power of his presence. Welcome him into your life today above all other loves.

MARCH 16

THE GIFT YOU HAVE

We all have something we feel most alive when doing. Call it a hobby, a talent, a passion—our niche. When we find that thing we both enjoy and excel in, it's one of the most special discoveries.

God has created us each with a unique skill set. He blessed us with talents that both distinguish us from others and complement us to others. He gave us these gifts so that we, as a whole created body of believers, could further his purposes and advance his kingdom.

> *Each of you should use whatever gift you have received to serve others, as faithful stewards of God's grace in its various forms (1 Peter 4:10, NIV).*

Think for a moment about the specific gifts God has given you. Don't be modest—God gives us gifts so that we can be confident in them for his glory! Now think about your gifts in direct relation to the kingdom of God. How can you use your gifts to benefit the church, the community, and the world? Seek to be an active participant in the kingdom of God using the tools that God specifically chose for you.

MARCH 17

GOVERNOR OF YOUR MIND

We think constantly about what we feed our bodies. Whether we eat healthy food or junk food, we are at least aware of what we are consuming. It's a simple principle: what you put in, you will get out. We know that if we continually feed ourselves junk food and candy, we will have low energy and poor health. We also know that if we eat balanced meals, we will feel better, look better, and function better.

Our thought patterns can easily be compared to our eating habits. When we fill our minds and hearts with things that aren't of God, our thoughts will follow those directions. Our thoughts determine our actions and our words. When we meditate on Scripture and fill our minds with Godly things, our thoughts, words, and actions will naturally be those of life, peace, and truth.

> *Those who are dominated by the sinful nature think about sinful things, but those who are controlled by the Holy Spirit think about things that please the Spirit. (Romans 8:5, NLT).*

What is governing your mind? Your flesh, or the Holy Spirit? Think carefully about what you put in, recognizing that it has a direct effect on what will come out.

MARCH 18

GRIEF

Grief is a strange thing. It shows up in the oddest of places. As time passes, it becomes threaded into your life in a subtle way you don't quite notice at first. When you smile and feel real joy but at the same moment tears spring to your eyes, that's when you know that grief is not absent even in happiness.

As time passes and life goes on, we must learn to bear all of our varying emotions in sync. We can smile, we can laugh, and we can be perfectly happy, but the ache of grief is still there deep down. We don't forget it, but we don't betray that which we grieve by smiling either.

Your promise revives me;
it comforts me in all my troubles (Psalm 119:50, NLT).

As a child of God, you have been promised a hope that has the power to revive you even in the most sorrowful of moments. And though your pain is real, deep, and sometimes overwhelming, your God is strong and able to lift you out of the deepest pit, and—even when it's hard to imagine—give you joy.

EACH NEW MORNING

There are many verses in the Bible that talk about morning prayer. Jesus himself set an example by getting up early and going to a quiet place to pray and talk with God. There is something about the morning that God values. Mornings symbolize new life, strong hope, and fresh beginnings—all things that we know God is passionate about.

When we seek God in the morning, we consecrate the first moments of the day. By coming and placing ourselves at his feet before we do anything else, we literally put him first in our hearts, souls, and minds.

Tell me in the morning about your love,
because I trust you.
Show me what I should do,
because my prayers go up to you (Psalm 143:8, NCV*).*

To start the day basking in the love of God is an amazing privilege. As we sit at his feet and read his Word, we gain strength, wisdom, direction, and perspective for the day ahead. Give him your day today. Find a quiet place to be in his presence and read his words of love to you. Listen to him tell you about his great affection toward you, and walk in that love as you face every obstacle and moment ahead.

MARCH 20

FROM WINTER TO SPRING

Spring teases us, playing its own game of "catch and release." A few balmy, sunny days awaken our senses to the freshness of spring air and promise the end of winter. We fall into bed after hours of sunshine and laughter, only to reawaken to a white blanket covering any evidence of warmth. Spring sun hides behind winter clouds, teasing us as though they know of our longing for the great light they hide. When the sun finally re-emerges, we are bathed in instant warmth.

Our lives have winters, don't they? We live through seasons where we feel cold, hidden, and trapped. We feel buried under the snow of circumstance with an absence of clarity, warmth, and light. But, if we looked closer, perhaps we could see the rushing of the clouds, the gilded outlines that promise there is hope just past them. And though winter can be long, the moment when the sun returns will be worth it all.

"Let us acknowledge the Lord;
let us press on to acknowledge him.
As surely as the sun rises,he will appear;
he will come to us like the winter rains,
like the spring rains that water the earth" (Hosea 6:3, NIV).

Perhaps you are in the midst of one of life's winters. Remember that for every winter there is a spring. For every woman, there is a strong God. As you press in to him, he will come to you like the sun rushing from behind the clouds. You have only to wait, to hope, and to look for him.

MARCH 21

IN HIS TIMING

Man can spend a lifetime studying God and never really understand the ways in which he moves: unexpected and unpredicted despite the prophecy of man, subtle yet monumental despite the theology of his character.

Abraham was told to look to the skies; his descendants would be as many as the stars. He was promised the future of mankind and a legacy that would shake history. Abraham was handed his dreams in one stunning moment by an almighty God. And then God was silent. All Abraham was left with was a barren, scoffing wife, a shocked expression, and an inky black sky filled with millions of stars representing impossible promise. But in his own timing, in his own way, God moved.

Rest in the Lord and wait patiently for Him….
Those who wait for the Lord, they will inherit the land (Psalm 37:7-9, NASB).

God has a timetable. You may feel like he has forgotten about you or that he's grown silent over the years. But God will honor the promises he's made to you. He will not forget to complete the work that he has begun. He has a master plan, and he will accomplish it. Be faithful even in the waiting and the quiet. At the right time, in the right way, he will move.

MARCH 22

RELATIONSHIPS

Humans were created for relationship; we are hardwired to want and need others. Because of our design, friendships are vitally important to our lives and also to our walk with God.

It is a widely known fact that friends either bring us up or drag us down. Likewise, friends can either encourage or discourage us in our pursuit of godliness. As we seek counsel from our friends for the decisions we make in life, it is important that those friends are pushing us to follow Christ and not our own desires.

Spend time with the wise and you will become wise,
but the friends of fools will suffer (Proverbs 13:20, NCV*).*

Your friends have the power to lead you closer to God or push you away from him. Surround yourself with people who will echo God's words to you rather than lead you off course with their advice. Evaluate yourself to make sure you are being the kind of friend who will lead others closer to Christ by your influence and your advice.

SCANDALOUS FORGIVENESS

There are few things worse than being unjustly wronged. It's not easy when you are hurt—especially by someone close to you. A deep part of each of us cries out for justice. It's a God-given trait, meant to call us to stand in the gap for the hurting, the widow, the orphan—it's our longing for true religion. When we identify injustice, that longing rises up strongly. We feel pain, hurt, confusion, and pressure. And more than all of those emotions, we feel the deep need to see justice served.

This is the scandal of the Gospel. This is the very essence of the Jesus we follow. Someone wrongs you? Forgive him. He wrongs you again? Forgive again. *But, Lord, he was wrong. He was sinful. He hurt me deeply.* His answer will still be the same: "Forgive, as I have forgiven you."

> *"Be on your guard! If your brother sins, rebuke him; and if he repents, forgive him. And if he sins against you seven times a day, and returns to you seven times, saying, 'I repent,' forgive him"* (Luke 17:3-4, NASB).

Beloved, we have been forgiven much; therefore, we must love much. No matter how hard it is today to forgive someone who has hurt you, remember how much you have been forgiven. How can we extend any less grace than that which we have received?

MARCH 24

FULLY ALIVE

Everyday living can suck the life right out of us. Somewhere in the middle of being stuck in traffic, sweeping floors, and brushing our teeth, we can forget to be alive.

What does it mean to be *alive*, rather than just to live? Not to only exist in life, but to know it, to understand it, to experience it—to *live* it. What would it be like? Freefalling from an airplane. Running through the grass barefoot with sun on your face. Bringing babies into the world, screaming and strong with power and life. What would it be like if we lived each moment in the spirit of those fully alive moments?

When you follow the revelation of the Word,
heaven's bliss fills your soul (Proverbs 29:18, TPT*).*

Without a reason for life, without purpose, we perish. We falter. We lose our way. We lose hope. We begin to casually exist instead of breathing in the reverence of a fully alive life. We need to re-cast vision for ourselves daily. Open your mind and your heart to the vision that God has for you. If there are dreams he gave you that you've lost along the way, trust that they will be returned to you. God breathed life into you so that you could live it to the fullest.

MARCH 25

NEVER TOO LATE

Do you have regrets in your life that you wish you could take back? Things that you aren't proud of? You lay awake at night thinking about mistakes you've made and you wonder if you've gone too far to ever get back.

When Jesus hung on the cross, there were two thieves hanging beside him. One of those thieves, as he hung in his final moments of life, asked Jesus for grace and a second chance. That thief—minutes before death—was given forgiveness and eternal life. The very same day he entered paradise as a forgiven and clean man. In light of his story, how can we ever say that it's too late to turn it all around?

Behold, the Lord's hand is not so short
That it cannot save;
Nor is His ear so dull
That it cannot hear (Isaiah 59:1, NASB*).*

If you feel like it's too late to change something in your life for the better, remember the story of the thief on the cross. There is always hope in Jesus. The God we serve is the God of second chances. That might sound cliché, but it couldn't be more true. His love has no end and his grace knows no boundary. It is never too late for you to follow him with your life.

MARCH 26

REBUILT

We were originally created to bear the mark of our Creator. We were masterfully designed to reflect his image and to reveal his glory. The corruption of sin has masked us, disguising our initial intended purpose. When we respond to salvation and give ourselves back to God, he begins reworking us to once again appear as he intended.

Sanctification is a process that can be painful. But its end result is beautiful. God empties our hearts of the things that could never satisfy to make room for himself—the only thing that will always satisfy.

From far away the Lord appeared to his people and said,
"I love you people
with a love that will last forever.
That is why I have continued
showing you kindness.
People of Israel, I will build you up again,
and you will be rebuilt.
You will pick up your tambourines again
and dance with those who are joyful"
(Jeremiah 31:3-4, NCV).

You may feel like God has taken a wrecking ball to your life. He has flattened everything you had—your desires, your interests, your pursuits—but *fear not*. He will rebuild you. He is creating a masterpiece with your life that will bring him glory and honor. Everything he removes he will restore to mirror the image of his likeness—your intended created purpose.

NEW LIFE

The entire human race is living on borrowed time. We spend our lives with the innate knowledge that we never know when it will all end for us. Death comes, as it always does, to every man.

When it came to Jesus, death didn't have the final say. And in that death—the one death that represented all humanity—the greatest form of life was born. The Gospel truth is that Jesus' death wasn't just a man's life ending on a cross. It was the death to literally end all deaths. Jesus died and took the full wrath of a righteous God upon himself so that our death sentences would no longer be ours to serve. And the story doesn't end there. The most glorious part of all is his resurrection: his conquering of death, and the ultimate display of power, glory, victory, and grace.

> *We died and were buried with Christ by baptism. And just as Christ was raised from the dead by the glorious power of the Father, now we also may live new lives (Romans 6:4, NLT).*

The whole point of the entire Gospel, summed up in one life giving phrase is this: you can have new life. Life that doesn't run out, expire, or end. This beautiful truth isn't just a charming thought. It's your reality as a Christian. By accepting the finished story of the Gospel, you are written into the best ending in existence. Life is yours—glorious, powerful life.

MARCH 28

HEAVEN'S PROMISE

When terrible things happen in this world, people cry out to God in desperation. They ask how he could have let it happen. How could the one who is in control of everything possibly be good when there is so much hardship?

But when we look at the system of heaven, we realize that God never intended for us to have sorrow, pain, or death. All of these things only exist as a result of man's sin. When the kingdom heaven is established on earth, we will live as God intended. All wrong will be righted and all pain will disappear.

> *"God will wipe away every tear from their eyes; there shall be no more death, nor sorrow, nor crying. There shall be no more pain, for the former things have passed away" (Revelation 21:4, NKJV).*

As a child of God, you know that any pain you have in this life is temporary because your eternal home will be devoid of it all. When the pain and sadness of the world threatens to overwhelm you, cling to the promise of heaven and the hope that one day every tear will be wiped from your eyes.

WHAT GOD DESIRES

As Christians who have knowingly received so much from God, we want to give something back. We see people around us who are giving back—they either have dedicated their lives to bringing the message of the Gospel to remote locations, or they are donors who fund entire ministries and give thousands to the poor. Surely these people are much further along than we are in the repayment of their debt to God.

These gifts are excellent. To go into the world is the great commission, and we know how important that is to Christ, and money can absolutely aid in advancing the kingdom here on earth…but are these the things that God really longs for?

My child, give me your heart,
and let your eyes observe my ways (Proverbs 23:26, NRSV).

More than anything extravagant that we wish we had to offer God, he wants the one thing we already have—ourselves. Christ didn't die on the cross so that we would faithfully tithe to our church, or sell everything we own for the sake of his name. He died simply to be with us, to make a way for us to know him and enter into pure relationship with him. Offer him yourself today.

MARCH 30

RENEWAL

Spring rains renew the earth; they wash the barren ground with life and new growth. The green they leave behind is the evidence of the power of their refreshment. Just as rain changes the earth at the turning of the seasons, so God changes the lives of men at the turning of their hearts.

No one who has truly encountered the presence of God can walk away unchanged. Full surrender of a life to Christ will be marked indelibly in that person's character. Jesus takes us as we are, but never leaves us as we were. His mission is always about taking back the lives that sin destroyed and making them new once more.

Anyone who belongs to Christ has become a new person. The old life is gone; a new life has begun!
(2 Corinthians 5:17, NLT)

God revives, rebuilds, recovers, and renews. He takes what was, strips it away, and creates something completely new. The incredible hope in this is that you don't have to attempt change alone. He will do the miraculous work of change in your life. He is doing a new thing—he has already begun!

WHAT IS YOUR FAITH WORTH?

As Christians, we are called to be the representation of Christ to the world; we are the visible expression of an invisible God. In order to express the heart of the Father, we have to know what is on his heart. God tells us in Scripture that he cares deeply about the "least of these": the orphan, the widow, the poor, the needy.

We cannot preach Christ to someone who is needy while leaving them in their need. Our words will not communicate the love of our Father unless accompanied by the actions that make him tangible to them.

> *If people say they have faith, but do nothing, their faith is worth nothing. Can faith like that save them? A brother or sister in Christ might need clothes or food. If you say to that person, "God be with you! I hope you stay warm and get plenty to eat," but you do not give what that person needs, your words are worth nothing (James 2:14-16, NCV).*

What is your faith worth? How far are you willing to go to express the love of God to a dying world? Will you give of yourself when it isn't convenient? Will you love on someone who is unlovable and give to someone who can never repay you? The cost may seem great, and the work insignificant, but God sees your heart and what you have done, and he counts it as work done directly for him.

APRIL

How enriched are they
who find their strength in the Lord;
within their hearts are the highways of holiness!
Even when their path winds
through the dark valley of tears,
they dig deep to find a pleasant pool
where others find only pain.
He gives to them a brook of blessing
filled from the rain of an outpouring.
They grow stronger and stronger
with every step forward
until they find all their strength in you.

Psalm 84:5-7 TPT

A SHINING EXAMPLE

When we accept the gift of Christ's salvation, we can be assured that we will live for eternity with our Father in heaven. There is nothing that we can do by our actions alone that ensures a place for us. But that doesn't mean the buck stops there. Though not a requirement for admittance through the pearly gates, a life lived doing good deeds is something every Christ follower should seek to attain.

As Christians, we are an extension of the Lord during our time on earth. Non-believers will be quick to point out our hypocrisy—let's not give them any reason to do so.

> *"In the same way, let your light shine before others, that they may see your good deeds and glorify your Father in heaven" (Matthew 5:16, NIV).*

Be a shining example of his love, so others can see how a life with Christ is a beautiful one. What is different about *your* life? Can others see that you love Christ by the choices you are making?

APRIL 2

CONSTANT COMPLAINT

The temptation to complain or bicker can be overwhelming at times. Get a group of women together in a room and you can almost see the tension grow. "She did this and it wasn't fair." "He doesn't contribute the way he should." "My life is hard for a multitude of reasons." The list can go on and on.

Our complaints are often valid and true, but we miss the joy that the Lord desires for us when we seek out only the negative.

> *Do everything without grumbling or arguing, so that you may become blameless and pure, "children of God without fault in a warped and crooked generation." Then you will shine among them like stars in the sky as you hold firmly to the word of life. And then I will be able to boast on the day of Christ that I did not run or labor in vain (Philippians 2:14-16,* NIV*).*

This letter from Paul to the Philippians was written thousands of years ago, but it could just have easily been written today. We still live in a warped and crooked generation. Let's shine like stars in the sky! Let us hold firmly to his Word as we speak life to those around us.

KEEPING A SECRET

We've all been there before. A friend leans in and whispers, "Did you hear about what *she* did?" And something in us wants to be in the know. To hear the scoop. To spread the word. It's almost as if we are built to be mean girls. To share what we know of others' downfalls and fallacies.

It might feel good in the moment to tear people down because then we are not alone in the many ways we fall short. But it is a lie. We were designed to lift one another up. To be worthy of knowing a friend's secrets because we will keep the knowledge to ourselves.

You can't trust a gossiper with a secret;
they'll just go blab it all.
Put your confidence instead in a trusted friend,
for he will be faithful to keep it in confidence
(Proverbs 11:13, TPT).

The next time you are tempted to share what isn't yours to tell, take a deep breath and pause. Ask yourself if betraying a confidence is worth letting down a friend. Instead, allow yourself to be the type of friend that the Lord has designed you to be.

APRIL 4

A WAY OUT

Each of us struggles with temptation. No one is exempt. From gossip to overindulging, to unkind thoughts, and more, we battle with temptation in all different ways.

The good news is that we serve a God who is faithful, and, oh, how he loves his children! The Bible tells us that he won't allow us to be faced with more than what we can handle. When we turn to him in the midst of our struggles, we can find our way out.

> *No temptation has overtaken you except what is common to mankind. And God is faithful; he will not let you be tempted beyond what you can bear. But when you are tempted, he will also provide a way out so that you can endure it (1 Corinthians 10:13,* NIV*).*

Be prepared for your time of battle by praying for protection. Ask the Lord to open your eyes to see the ways in which you may fall, so that you can be ready to face them head on. Though temptation will surely come your way, be assured that it will not overcome you as you trust in the Lord in all you do.

HE HEARS

Sometimes it can feel as if God is far away: an elusive man in the heavens who is so far above us that surely he cannot be interested in our day-to-day lives. Our desires and requests seem so small by comparison that it seems unworthy a task to even ask him for help.

But he is a God who loves his children. He wants us to be happy, to feel fulfilled. When we approach him with our wants and needs, he truly hears us! The next time you feel as if your requests are too unimportant to bother God about, remind yourself that he is always listening. Though he may not answer you in the way you expect, he is right there beside you, ready to lend an ear.

> *This is the confidence we have in approaching God: that if we ask anything according to his will, he hears us. And if we know that he hears us—whatever we ask—we know that we have what we asked of him (1 John 5:14-15, NIV).*

Allow yourself to be filled with God's presence today. He loves you and wants the best for you. If you ask in his will, he will answer you.

APRIL 6

ONLY A HEART CHANGE

It's easy to feel compassion for those who suffer. You see the unfairness of it all—good people who are struggling with the pressures of what life has thrown their way. But what about those people who don't seem so "good"? The ones you look at and say, "Well, they deserve some suffering for all the wrong they've done." It's tough to look into our hearts and find compassion for them, but the Bible tells us we must do so anyway!

Our God is kind to the ungrateful and wicked; therefore, we must be too. Though it goes against our very nature to do good to those who have wronged us, it is expected of us. This requires nothing short of a heart change that can only come from the Lord.

> *"Love your enemies, do good to them, and lend to them without expecting to get anything back. Then your reward will be great, and you will be children of the Most High, because he is kind to the ungrateful and wicked. Be merciful, just as your Father is merciful"* (Luke 6:35-36, NIV).

Pray for a change of heart today! Ask your heavenly Father to soften your heart toward those who do you harm. Only then can you truly love your enemies the way he wants you to.

CHILDISH BEHAVIOR

It can often be difficult to obey God. Even as grown women, everything in us sometimes wants us to stomp our feet and shout, "No!" When life throws hard tasks our way, we want to flee. We want to submit to our own desires and ignore what God is asking of us.

But that leaves us incomplete. Scripture says that obedience will make us whole in our relationship with God. We will truly know what love means when we choose obedience. And we cannot claim to know him and love him if we are not living by his Word.

> *If anyone obeys his word, love for God is truly made complete in them. This is how we know we are in him: Whoever claims to live in him must live as Jesus did (1 John 2:5-6,* NIV*).*

When the child in you threatens to rise up and make choices for you, stop and pray. Lean in closer to the Lord and ask him for his help in choosing obedience. It's only with his guidance that we are able to be made complete and leave the foot stomping to the little ones.

APRIL 8

AWAKENING THE SUN

April is a gorgeous time of year in the northern region of the world. Snow is melting, buds are opening, and the earth appears to be coming back to life after a deep slumber.

Just as we appreciate the beauty of the season, God has a fine eye for loveliness too. He is the ultimate painter, creating a beautiful canvas all over the world as it awakes. He wants each of us to be embraced in the warmth of the sun as we are reminded of his warmth and love.

What a heavenly home God has set for the sun,
shining in the superdome of the sky!
See how he leaves his celestial chamber each morning,
radiant as a bridegroom ready for his wedding,
like a day-breaking champion eager to run his course.
He rises on one horizon, completing his circuit on the
other, warming lives and lands with his heat
(Psalm 19:4-6, TPT*).*

Look up! Turn your face toward the sun. Let its warmth come over you. God is working in all things—even through the sunshine. Just as its light touches every corner of the earth, the Lord is working in every area of your life. Allow him to do his work in you today. Take time to notice the ways in which he is touching you with his warm embrace.

MOST BEAUTIFUL OF ALL

If there is one thing that a woman can appreciate, it's something pretty. Shiny things easily catch our attention, and we seek to surround ourselves with beauty. There is much beauty to be found in our natural world.

There is nothing wrong with finding *loveliness* in our world, but if there is one thing that is more beautiful than anything else, it is the Lord God himself. His love, his mercy, his grace, and his understanding—it is nothing short of breathtaking.

Here's the one thing I crave from God,
the one thing I seek above all else:
I want the privilege of living with him
every moment in his house,
finding the sweet loveliness of his face,
filled with awe, delighting in his glory and grace.
I want to live my life so close to him
that he takes pleasure in my every prayer (Psalm 27:4, TPT).

Don't miss the beauty of the Lord today. Seek it. It's there to be found! You've been created to enjoy all that is exquisite, beautiful, and captivating. Give in to that desire, and find it in him! Once you have discovered the allure of it, you will find that nothing is more handsome than the Lord in his love.

APRIL 10

CHECKLIST

It's easy to go about our day, crossing our many to-do items off our lists and making sure we accomplish all of our tasks. Sometimes, spending time with the Lord can become just another box to check off. Toilets? Cleaned. Groceries? Purchased. Scripture reading? Check.

But the Lord wants so much more out of his relationship with us than to be merely another chore to accomplish or another bullet point on our checklist. He is so much more than a small portion of your day, forgotten after you've closed your Bible. Search for him—he wants to be found! He wants to show you all that can be had when you desire true relationship with him.

You will seek me and find me when you seek me with all your heart (Jeremiah 29:13, NIV).

Are you holding back in your relationship with the Lord, or have you given him all of your heart? Don't reserve anything. Give all of yourself to him! Seek him in all areas of your life. He is there wherever you look, waiting for you, wanting to connect with you.

LOSING TO WIN

Selfish. The word itself is an ugly one. It brings to mind all that is unflattering inside. There is no denying that we want, first and foremost, what's best for *us* in life. What's best for others? Well, that is secondary.

But for the life of a Christian? That calls for something else entirely. Scripture plainly says that we are not to put ourselves first, but instead must lose our life for one in Christ. If we try to hang on to our selfish ways, we will lose our lives. But we are saved when we take up our cross and follow him instead. When we say no to the flesh, we say yes to so much more.

> *"Whoever wants to be my disciple must deny themselves and take up their cross and follow me. For whoever wants to save their life will lose it, but whoever loses their life for me and for the gospel will save it" (Mark 8:34-35,* NIV*).*

Take a look at your life today. In what areas have you become wrapped up in yourself? Give those areas to the Lord, and seek his will for your life.

APRIL 12

ENEMY TACTIC

The more you dive into your relationship with the Lord, the more the enemy will want to pull you away. The more you begin to listen for God's voice, the more Satan will try to whisper in your ear. Allowing yourself to become closer to God is the last thing the enemy wants for you.

You're not good enough. Nothing is going right for you. You're making all the wrong decisions. These lies may play over and over again in your head until they start to sound like reality. Suddenly, you find yourself believing them all. This isn't what the Lord wants for you! He wants you to be glad in him.

Let them all be glad,
those who turn aside to hide themselves in you.
May they keep shouting for joy forever!
Overshadow them in your presence
as they sing and rejoice,
then every lover of your name will burst forth
with endless joy (Psalm 5:11, TPT).

Pray for protection from the lies the enemy wants you to believe. Ask the Lord to speak in a voice that is loud enough to hear through the deception. He wants to rejoice with you; he wants what's best for you. Trust in that knowledge today as you spend time with him.

APRIL 13

BORN FOR RELATIONSHIP

Before the human race ever came into existence, there was relationship. The Father, Son, and Holy Spirit co-existed in a loving bond with one another. They were interdependent, in need of connection with others. They were the very first example of what it means to feel kinship.

Because we were created in God's image, we were made for relationship with each other. We crave it. Scripture tells us that it isn't good for us to be alone, so why is it that we often feel so lonely? We can be standing in a room full of people, and feel no connection with any one of them.

The LORD God said, "It is not good for the man to be alone" (Genesis 2:18 NIV).

If you feel lonely, take stock of the ways in which you have put up walls to prevent true friendship from happening. Are you getting in your own way of developing strong bonds with others? Pray that the Lord will place people in your life that will be a source of authentic relationship. Seek ways to mature these connections beginning today!

APRIL 14

MOUNTAIN MOVERS

Matthew 17:20 tells us that if we have faith as small as a mustard seed, we can literally move mountains. Since none of us have plans to pick up Mount Kilimanjaro and find a new spot for it, how can we apply this knowledge to our own lives? Truly, it sounds a bit wacky that we can do great things with only a little faith. And yet scripture tells us that it's so!

How can we step out in faith? It looks different for everyone. For some, the first step may be giving themselves fully to a belief that Christ died for their sins. For others, it could look like jumping out of a job that isn't a good fit and taking a leap into the unknown, or giving up a toxic relationship knowing that the Lord will be there to take care of them.

> *Without faith it is impossible to please God, because anyone who comes to him must believe that he exists and that he rewards those who earnestly seek him (Hebrews 11:6, NIV).*

Seek his will for your life today. How does he want you to take a leap? What does it look like in your own life? Spend some time reflecting on this today—he wants to reward you for your faith!

GENTLE RESTORATION

It's hard to watch someone we love start to spiral into a cycle of poor choices. Everything in us wants to tell them to snap out of it, to shake them and ask why they just can't see that what they're doing is wrong.

But the Bible says that we should restore them gently. In love. The very definition of the word *restore* is to repair. To properly repair something, you must take care to give it the support it needs. You can't just slap a nail on a broken cabinet and expect it to hold up. It may work for a while, but without taking all the necessary steps to bring it back to its original condition, it will only deteriorate once again over time.

If someone is caught in a sin, you who live by the Spirit should restore that person gently. But watch yourselves, or you also may be tempted (Galatians 6:1, NIV*).*

Do you know someone who needs restoration? Ask God to show you how you can gently support them through it. Pray for protection for yourself so that you will not fall into the same trap.

APRIL 16

UNDER HIS WING

At some point, each of us feels hurt. We feel pain that goes beyond what we think we can bear, that pushes us to the brink of what we think we can handle, that leaves us bruised and brokenhearted. And we can feel so *alone* in our grief.

There is someone who is always with us, ready to give us comfort. Jesus doesn't want us to live in pain. He wants to give us refuge. We may not know why we are bearing our particular burden. It often feels unfair, but we need to know that we can go to him in the midst of it and find relief.

> *His massive arms are wrapped around you, protecting you.*
> *You can run under his covering of majesty and hide.*
> *His arms of faithfulness are a shield keeping you from harm*
> *(Psalm 91:4, TPT).*

Give your pain to God. Cry out to him. He wants to give you peace. Let him take you under his wing and shelter you from all that hurts you. Show him your wounds and allow him to heal them today. Rest in the knowledge that you are never alone.

ME FIRST

What is the first thing everyone does when they see a group picture in which they were included? They look at themselves, right? They check to make sure their hair looked good, their lipstick wasn't smudged, that they were positioned so as to get the most flattering angle.

We are, to put it bluntly, quite self-centered. Our first thought is of ourselves. But what would happen if we chose to view others in the picture first? What if we first admired the others in the picture? In the greater picture of life, are we thinking of ourselves first, or are we putting others before us?

Do not seek your own advantage, but that of the other (1 Corinthians 10:24, NRSV*).*

The Lord has asked us to think of others before ourselves. It's easy to make sure our needs are served before we look at others. What are the ways in which you can seek to serve other people before yourself today?

APRIL 18

FEAR OR FRIGHT?

Sometimes we think of God as being full of fire and brimstone, doom and gloom. We learn that we should have a fear of the Lord, and suddenly our God becomes a scary one.

There is a significant difference between a healthy fear and being afraid. Though we commonly associate the words fear and fright with one another they don't mean the same thing. Having a fear of the Lord means we respect him. It means we are in awe of him. He is, in fact, a God of great joy. When we seek to be fully in his presence, we can find that joy.

You will show me the path of life;
In your presence is fullness of joy;
At your right hand are pleasures forevermore
(Psalm 16:11, NKJV).

Our Father wants you to experience his joy! Pleasures forevermore? Let's sign up for that! Shake off any old notions of dread or apprehension you may feel about being in his presence, and seek the path of life he has set for you. He is a source of great delight! Rejoice in that knowledge today.

CLEAR OUT THE CLUTTER

Springtime is a great time to clear out the clutter and give your home a redo. It feels good to be able to sift through everything you've been hanging on to, and get rid of the things that aren't working for you anymore. That pile of things to be donated shows the progress you made.

In the same way that our homes need to be cleared of all the useless items we collect over the years, our souls can use a good refreshing too. Over the years, we collect bad habits, wrongful ways of thinking, and relics of our old lifestyles—ones that no longer fit our lives.

Start over with me, and create a new,
clean heart within me.
Fill me with pure thoughts and holy desires,
ready to please you.
May there never be even a shadow of darkness between us!
May you never deprive me of your Sacred Spirit
(Psalm 51:10-11, TPT).

It's time to sift through your heart! What are you hanging onto that doesn't fit with how you want to live your life now? Why are you keeping it around? Make a pile of the spiritual clutter. Stack it up, take one last look, and then be done with it. Progress is a beautiful thing!

APRIL 20

TOSSED BY WAVES

There's nothing quite like the feeling of riding on a boat on a beautiful day. It's incredibly relaxing, leaning back and enjoying the gentle rocking of the waves. But have you ever been out on the water during a storm? It's anything but relaxing. In fact, being tossed around by dangerous winds as the waves grow larger is downright scary.

When James paints a picture of what happens when we doubt, it should be taken seriously. After all, his generation definitely knew what it was like to be at sea. They depended on fishing for much of what they ate! And with none of today's technology and gear to save them from a storm, the danger was very real.

> *When you ask, you must believe and not doubt, because the one who doubts is like a wave of the sea, blown and tossed by the wind (James 1:6,* NIV*).*

Pray for wisdom! But when you do, make sure you are ready to receive it. Believe the word that the Lord has for you, and do not doubt. Your very life depends on it.

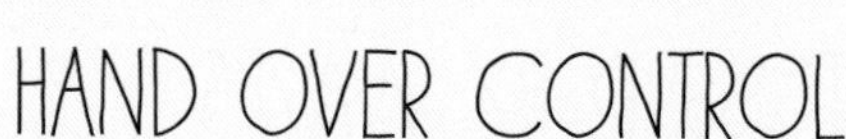

HAND OVER CONTROL

The phone rings, and with it, your heart sinks. It's the bad news you've been dreading. The news that could make you question everything you know. Suddenly, you're in the midst of a struggle. Why would the Lord allow such terrible things to happen if he truly loved us?

Trust is a tricky thing. When you fully trust someone, you completely give yourself over to them. And when you fully trust God, you allow him to take the reins of your life and give him all the control. You're no longer in the driver's seat—you're an active passenger, riding shotgun. And though it's difficult, giving of yourself completely means that you don't have to fear the bad that will inevitably come. He's got it, in his very capable hands.

They will have no fear of bad news;
their hearts are steadfast, trusting in the Lord.
Their hearts are secure, they will have no fear;
in the end they will look in triumph on their foes
(Psalm 112:7-8, NIV).

Have you given control of your life completely over to God, or are you the passenger who can't help but give directions during the ride? Release your worries and cares to him today and allow him to carry your burden for you. He is strong enough to handle it!

APRIL 22

PRIZE OF GLORY

As Christians, we are told that we are God's children. Scripture confirms this for us, so we know it to be true. As his children, we can rest in the knowledge that we are set to inherit all that is his.

While that doesn't exempt us from going through rough patches, the good news is that Scripture also tells us that we get to share in his glory. And that is excellent news indeed. Glory isn't just something nice like a sunny day or a delicious piece of chocolate. It's downright fabulous. *Resplendent beauty* and *magnificence* are just a couple of ways to describe it.

> *The Spirit himself testifies with our spirit that we are God's children. Now if we are children, then we are heirs—heirs of God and co-heirs with Christ, if indeed we share in his sufferings in order that we may also share in his glory (Romans 8:16-17,* NIV*).*

Imagine the most beautiful place you've ever been, or the most amazing moment you've ever experienced. It pales in comparison to the glory of the Lord—and we get to share it! Rejoice in that today. Though you may experience suffering along the way, sharing in his glory is the best prize you could ever receive.

CALL ON HIM

All too often we can find ourselves, in our very full and busy lives, utterly alone. We feel misunderstood, an outcast of our doing. We isolate ourselves in a world of pain, feeling as though there is no one to whom we can turn.

There is good news! There is someone who always answers when we call. God is waiting for us to call upon him. He has enough love to go around—enough for anybody willing to seek it out. We cry for mercy, and he hears our cries.

Have mercy on me, Lord, for I call to you all day long.
Bring joy to your servant, Lord, for I put my trust in you.
You, Lord, are forgiving and good,
abounding in love to all who call to you.
Hear my prayer, LORD; listen to my cry for mercy.
When I am in distress, I call to you,
because you answer me (Psalm 86:3-7, NIV).

Whatever you are going through, call on him for support today. Scripture says he is forgiving and good. He wants to love you through your pain, and bring you out of your misery. He will answer you if you are willing to ask him for help.

APRIL 24

TRUE WORSHIP

When was the last time you gave yourself over fully to a time of worship? Not just singing along to the words in church, not just bowing your head in prayer, but letting yourself be completely consumed by the presence of the Lord?

True worship is quite different than just singing along. We serve a God who is awesome and powerful. He is deserving of our utmost devotion. When we discover just how amazing he is, we know that he is worth our full praise.

> *"A time is coming and has now come when the true worshipers will worship the Father in the Spirit and in truth, for they are the kind of worshipers the Father seeks. God is spirit, and his worshipers must worship in the Spirit and in truth" (John 4:23-24,* NIV*).*

Let's be the kind of worshipers that our Father seeks! Take some quiet time today to allow his mighty presence to wash over you, filling every crevice of your being. Revel in the time that you have with him, worshiping him in whatever way feels natural to you. You'll discover that he is indeed worthy of your adoring reverence.

STRUGGLING TO PRAY

Do you ever sit down to pray and find yourself struggling to find the words to begin? You stumble over your words, your mind draws a blank. You want to be obedient by spending time with the Lord, but you don't even know where to begin.

The good news is that God intervenes for us in the midst of every type of struggle, including our prayer life. He's got our back in times of pain and misery. Why wouldn't he be there for us when we want to converse with him? He will give us the words to say when we find ourselves lacking. In fact, he will even go beyond that and give you a form of communication that words can't express!

> *He is able also to save forever those who draw near to God through Him, since He always lives to make intercession for them (Hebrews 7:25,* NASB*).*

When you find yourself searching for the right way to express what you want to say to God, know that he will intercede if you allow him to. Spend some time sitting quietly, and let him takes the reins for you today. He knows your heart!

APRIL 26

THE FOXES

Foxes are known for their cunning. They're sneaky little things, hunting their prey on the sly. They're known for their ability to camouflage themselves, hiding as they circle, and then suddenly pouncing on their intended target. And then, they use their teeth to sink in, shaking their catch until the life recedes from them.

Our enemy is a cunning one, and he uses our sin and temptations in the same sly way. They're camouflaged in the corners of our minds where we don't even notice until it's often too late. We see it when we're already caught, and our sin is shaking us to the point where we're ready to give up and give in.

Catch for us the foxes,
the little foxes
that ruin the vineyards,
our vineyards that are in bloom (Song of Songs 2:15, NIV*).*

God wants us to be like vineyards that are in bloom. He's ready to catch the foxes that are our would-be predators. Look for the ways that sin might be hiding in your heart, and give it over to the Lord so that he can prevent the unnecessary shaking in your life.

APRIL 27

A DISCIPLINE OF TIME

Self-discipline is a tough one to master, especially when it comes to spending daily time with the Lord. It's easy to find an excuse not to take that quiet time with him. You've got a full schedule ahead of you. Mornings are crazy, but nights get busy too. There's never a convenient time to check it off your list.

When we truly experience God in the way he desires, it becomes about more than just another item on our to-do list. Just as someone who trains for a marathon must be disciplined to spend time running regularly, we must train ourselves to spend time with our Father. Once it becomes our habit, it also becomes our joy.

> *Do you not know that in a race all the runners run, but only one gets the prize? Run in such a way as to get the prize. Everyone who competes in the games goes into strict training. They do it to get a crown that will not last, but we do it to get a crown that will last forever*
> *(1 Corinthians 9:24-25, NIV).*

We are all running in this race called life. Let's not let our eyes be drawn away from the greatest prize of all: a crown that will last forever.

APRIL 28

CHORUS OF LOVE

Oh, the many ways in which we sin! We are full of mistakes. We make so many poor choices. The list of ways in which we fall short is endless.

If we are truly repentant, we don't need to spend time beating ourselves up over the mistakes we make. We get to say we're sorry and then move on. Scripture tells us that the Lord takes great delight in us! When Jesus died to save us from our sins, there was no longer need for rebuke. Instead, he rejoices over us with singing! Can you imagine? The very God who saved us is so thrilled about it that he sings us a song.

"The LORD your God is with you,
the Mighty Warrior who saves.
He will take great delight in you;
in his love he will no longer rebuke you,
but will rejoice over you with singing" (Zephaniah 3:17, NIV).

Listen to the chorus that the Lord has for you. The very fact that you exist gives him great pleasure. Repent of your sin, and rejoice with him today! He wants to sing *with* you.

BLESSED

When Mary, a virgin, was told that she was going to have a baby—the son of God no less—she must've felt a huge range of emotions. If she was anything like us, she probably felt quite a bit of fear and trepidation. I'm sure she wondered what her soon-to-be husband would think of her story. Like women still do today, she rushed to a trusted friend in whom she could confide.

What's the first thing her friend and cousin Elizabeth says to her? That she was *blessed*. She believed that God would follow through on what he told her was true, and because of that, she was endowed with divine favor. This gift she would be given wasn't one she asked for, and she'd have to face a great deal of hardship because of it, but she believed that God was good through it all.

> *"Blessed is she who has believed that the Lord would fulfill his promises to her!"* (Luke 1:45, NIV).

Are you looking for God's promises amidst your hardship? Believe that what the Lord says is true, and you, too, will find blessings in your own life.

APRIL 30

EXTENT OF GOD'S LOVE

Paul's letter written to the Ephesians was a powerful prayer that sprang from his deep desire to see the people living a life that was only achieved with total commitment to Christ. He believed that it was worth the struggle that often came with living this way, because the reward was great.

This letter could've been written to each and every one of us. When we feel Christ's indwelling in our hearts, we can experience true power, and true love.

> *For this reason I kneel before the Father, from whom every family in heaven and on earth derives its name. I pray that out of his glorious riches he may strengthen you with power through his Spirit in your inner being, so that Christ may dwell in your hearts through faith. And I pray that you, being rooted and established in love, may have power, together with all the Lord's holy people, to grasp how wide and long and high and deep is the love of Christ, and to know this love that surpasses knowledge—that you may be filled to the measure of all the fullness of God (Ephesians 3:14-19,* NIV*).*

Have you experienced how wide, long, high, and deep God's love is for you? He wants you to feel it in its fullness. Pray for that today!

The happiest people on earth
are those who worship you with songs.
They firmly march along shouting with joy and
shining in the radiance streaming from your face.
We can do nothing but leap for joy all day long;
for we know who you are and what you do,
and you've exalted us on high.

Psalm 89:15-16 TPT

MAY 1

OVERFLOW OF ANGER

Where does the flashing overflow of anger come from? Or the tendency to hold a grudge, or give the cold shoulder? Shouting, huffing, slamming, seething… anger begins somewhere deep inside us where we've been offended. Or disrespected. Or maybe mistreated.

Whatever the origin, anger is very difficult to control and the enemy preys on our weak flesh and wounded ego to destroy us. Prideful anger is an expression of our selfish desires: *How dare they make my life difficult? They should know better than to get in the way of my ease and pleasure!*

We are called, beloved sisters, to walk in the love and peace of Jesus Christ, and to bear witness to his righteousness:

> *You, O Lord, are a God full of compassion, and gracious,*
> *Longsuffering and abundant in mercy and truth*
> *(Psalm 86:15, NKJV).*

When anger threatens to overcome your compassion, remember God's devotion to you and his unending love. Despite your sin, he is long-suffering and gracious. If you submit your offenses to God and extend grace by his Holy Spirit, the harmful flames of anger are reduced to ash. His holy mercy washes them away, leaving your heart cleansed and your mind renewed.

ROYALTY PROTOCOL

Imagine walking into Buckingham Palace, unnoticed and unrestricted, without knocking or announcing yourself, and pulling up a chair alongside Her Majesty, the Queen of England. "I've had such a long day. Nothing has gone right, and now my car is making the strangest noise. Could you help me out?"

Such an image is almost absurd! There is a protocol to seeing royalty—many rules to follow, not to mention the armed guards protecting every side. But there is a royal throne we can approach without fear or proper etiquette. It is without guards, payments, locks, and restrictions. Its occupant is the God of all creation, and he is eager to hear about your day's ups and downs.

Let us come boldly to the throne of our gracious God. There we will receive his mercy, and we will find grace to help us when we need it most (Hebrews 4:16, NLT).

Approach the throne, shamelessly pull up a chair, and lift your voice to him. He loves your company. What do you need? Ask him without fear. What gifts has he given? Thank him in person. What guidance are you looking for? His wisdom is yours if you will listen.

TOXIC THINKING

Sometimes while driving, little annoyances can spur us into a prideful mindset: we're the only ones driving at a safe speed, or signaling correctly, or paying attention to the rules of the road. *Why doesn't anyone else know what they're doing?!* The small things escalate quickly and suddenly we're out of control, figuratively speaking.

It's pride, plain and simple. *I have it all figured out and everyone else needs to get with it.* This kind of thinking is not only unpleasant for those around us, it's toxic to the soul. And it spreads quickly!

It's best to set the mind on Christ and his reconciliation… and set it quickly before we start condemning friends and family, too! In Christ, we're all just doing our best to get where we need to go. We're not superior to anyone. We're not too terrible either because God created us and sent his Son Jesus to die for us. This makes us worthy.

> *We are made right with God by placing our faith in Jesus Christ. And this is true for everyone who believes, no matter who we are. For everyone has sinned; we all fall short of God's glorious standard (Romans 3:22-23,* NLT*).*

Think on this today, whether you're on the road or not. Pray you'll arrive safely wherever you're going, and maybe try a pleasant wave to others on the way there.

DARE TO HOPE

Do you know *whose* you are? Your father and mother rightly claim you as their child, but do you recognize Jesus as the one who also calls you his daughter? He knows your coming and going, and your every inner working. You are his.

How difficult it is to put our needs into the hands of the Father! Do we dare hope? Imagine watching a child die and feeling the despair of her absence, as the father of the girl in the story of Luke must have done. Then Jesus claims that she is only asleep! Both the girl's father and Jesus love the child, and both can claim her as their daughter, but only Jesus commands her spirit and her life. His child hears his voice and obeys his command.

> *"Stop wailing," Jesus said. "She is not dead but asleep." They laughed at him, knowing that she was dead. But he took her by the hand and said, "My child, get up!" Her spirit returned, and at once she stood up. Then Jesus told them to give her something to eat (Luke 8:52-55,* NIV*).*

God is faithful to the deepest needs of your heart; he knows you full well! Where is he directing you today? Are you a daughter in need of healing? Of hope? Hear his voice and let your spirit be renewed!

MAY 5

DRINK FROM THE RIVER

It happens on occasion, when the heavy spring rains come, that some homeowners find themselves on hands and knees trying to staunch the flow of water into their basement. The water rushes in, not down from the walls or windows, but up from the rising water table and through the foundation. And the owners bow low, soaking up all that they can.

It's a trying time, to be sure, as patience wears thin and towels pile high. But remember the living water, which springs up and gives life to the full! We can remind ourselves to draw abundantly from these waters in times of frustration.

God, your love is so precious!
You protect people in the shadow of your wings.
They eat the rich food in your house,
and you let them drink from your river of pleasure.
You are the giver of life.
Your light lets us enjoy life (Psalm 36:7-9, NCV).

It's painful to be tested. But the heart soars, and all thirsts are satisfied. You are in the company of Jesus Christ, who came not to be served, but to serve. Can you think of any better place to be? Let his love fill you up to overflowing with gratitude and praise.

ALWAYS CARING

When the hospital doors slide open and we aren't sure what news will greet us, God is compassionate. When the boss calls us for a meeting and dismissal is a real possibility, God is gentle. When we return home late at night to find our personal treasures stolen or destroyed, God is comforting. He cares so deeply for us.

Some see God as distant, vengeful, or condemning. Others see God as kind, affectionate, and attentive. Sometimes circumstances become too overwhelming. Mountains of anxiety rise up and we feel isolated and alone.

Let no doubt take root; he is a God who cares deeply, loves fully, and remains faithful, ever at our side in times of trouble. Though our sorrows overwhelm us, he is the comfort that we need.

> *When you go through deep waters and great trouble, I will be with you. When you go through rivers of difficulty, you will not drown! When you walk through the fire of oppression, you will not be burned up—the flames will not consume you (Isaiah 43:2,* TLB*).*

Will you take his hand, offered in love, and receive his comforting touch? Will you remember his faithfulness and let it calm your heart? He is with you! You will not drown! The flames will not consume you! Cling to his promises, and the mountains, as high as they may seem, will crumble at your feet.

MAY 7

STEADFAST PATH

There is a Family Circus cartoon where the son is asked to take out the garbage. The drawing then traces the tangled and erratic pathway between the boy and his final destination. He bounces over couches, through windows, under wheelbarrows, around trees, between siblings, all on the way to the curb-side trash can.

Our lives can feel like this at times: unpredictable, illogical, and inconsistent. Changes in work, marriage, family, or church can make the road seem irrational, uneven, and confusing. But God makes us the promise of a steadfast path when we keep his covenant. When we consider our lives through our limited human perspective, the path seems wavering. But the guidance of Jesus Christ is, in fact, steadfast!

All the paths of the Lord are steadfast love and faithfulness, for those who keep his covenant and his testimonies (Psalm 25:10, ESV).

Your path has been chosen for you and your feet have been set upon it. Truly, it is a path of love and faithfulness. He has made a covenant with you and you keep it when you trust him—even in the refinement of your path. It will be uncomfortable at times and you might ask yourself why his guidance is winding you around in the craziest of directions, but trust him! His paths are perfect.

EVERY TALENT COUNTS

During World War I, the American Red Cross called on American citizens to assist the troops fighting overseas. One of their greatest successes was a knitting campaign called *Knit Your Bit*, which required only knitting needles, wool, and an easily-learned skill. At the end of the war, Americans had produced 24 million military garments, including sweaters, helmet-liners, and socks. Men, women, boys, and girls all contributed to the effort. No skill was too little, no contribution too insignificant, to answer the call.

In the same way, your creative skills are a gift to the kingdom of God. Your imagination can be used for his glory! You may think God isn't interested in using your creativity. But your gifts are a great blessing to others. Where might your efforts be a blessing? Do you know someone who could benefit from your thoughtfulness? Your humble offerings bear witness of God's love!

> *The Lord has given them special skills as engravers, designers, embroiderers in blue, purple, and scarlet thread on fine linen cloth, and weavers. They excel as craftsmen and as designers (Exodus 35:35, NLT).*

Perhaps you have the desire but believe you lack the skill. Take lessons from video tutorials to help you develop the God-given desire and creativity you already possess into a talent that he promises to use. It is for his glory that we are given talents; prayerfully consider how to grow and use yours for his purposes.

A HIGHER VANTAGE POINT

In times of war, army strategists benefit from high vantage points. Looking upon the battlefield from above is the best way to formulate strategies for their troops. Before the use of satellite equipment and heat-sensing radar, views were limited to ground level, forcing strategists to use whatever maps and spies they could to predict enemy movement and position their men.

In the same way, our lives benefit from a higher viewpoint. When we rise above our circumstances and see life not from our own anxious, urgent, overwhelming perspective but from God's, life's battles become less intimidating as eternity's promises rise into view.

God has plans for our lives, but sometimes they are hard to see. The day-to-day defeats of life consume us and we struggle to confidently lift our head above the fray. When this happens, we can remember his high thoughts and ways, and believe that he will lead us through. He can see the entire battlefield, when we can only see our private foxhole and the crushing explosions that surround us.

Victory comes from you, O Lord.
May you bless your people (Psalm 3:8, NLT).

What does it look like for you to trust God in the battle today? You can be confident that he will lead you safely to victory.

HELD CAPTIVE BY FEAR

A pilot watches the flashing red light. A mother searches frantically for her child between the aisles. A driver glances in the rearview mirror at an oncoming truck. Certain fears have a gripping embrace, paralyzing to the body. The heart pounds, pupils dilate, palms sweat.

Other fears overwhelm the mind, causing anxious thoughts and sleepless nights. How will the bills get paid this month? Will the doctor have bad news? Family members need help, friends are overwhelmed with suffering, and we can't make it all okay.

When fearful thoughts flood our minds, God's words of wisdom and comfort can get washed away. If we can learn to fully trust him, he will calm our fears and still our quickened hearts. We can be fearless because our confidence is in God and his promises.

When you lie down, you will not be afraid;
Yes, you will lie down and your sleep will be sweet.
Do not be afraid of sudden terror,
Nor of trouble from the wicked when it comes;
For the LORD will be your confidence,
And will keep your foot from being caught
(Proverbs 3:24-26, NKJV).

What fears are holding you captive today? Let the flood of terror subside and be assured that God is your refuge. He lovingly attends to your every need. Do not be afraid!

MAY 11

TEMPER TANTRUMS

Temper tantrums are as common for adults as they are for children; they just look different in action. Children haven't learned to curb the screaming and stomping of frustration or anger, while adults have more restrained behavior. But the heart is the same, and the reactions stem from the same provocation.

James cuts right to the heart of sin. We want what we want but we don't have it, so we throw a tantrum. It's amazing how simple it is! Watch a child and this truth will play out soon enough. Watch an adult, and it may be more difficult to discern, but unfortunately it is there in all of us.

Praise God for his amazing grace, which is extended to us for this very reason. Let us submit to God's forgiveness and draw near to him for his cleansing and purifying grace. It washes over us, and our tantrums are forgiven. When we humble ourselves, he promises to exalt us. What more could we want?

> *What is causing the quarrels and fights among you? Don't they come from the evil desires at war within you? You want what you don't have, so you scheme and kill to get it. You are jealous of what others have, but you can't get it, so you fight and wage war to take it away from them (James 4:1-2,* NLT*).*

Do you see responses in yourself that remind you of a child throwing a tantrum? God's forgiveness is bigger than all of that. Thank him today for his mercy and grace. He loves it when you dwell on that.

MAY 12

NEW LIFE

Spring is a time of rebirth and renewal, a reward for making it through the long, cold, desolate winter. Some parts of the world have enjoyed colorful spring gardens in full fragrant bloom for weeks. In other regions, the cold snow is still melting and the earliest bulbs have yet to reach through the hard soil. Whether above the surface or below, resurrection is happening all around us, rewarding us with new life and vitality. Resurrection is a revival of hope, of light shining in the darkness, of our glorious reward.

Isaiah 42:16 shares a promise that cannot be taken away from us. He has achieved his glory and we will share in its reward: death cannot conquer or steal our inheritance! Therefore, we can fully trust and believe in Jesus Christ, our hope. There is nothing more magnificent, nothing else worthy of our expectations, for he has made a way for us to share in his glory!

I will bring the blind by a way they did not know;
I will lead them in paths they have not known.
I will make darkness light before them,
And crooked places straight.
These things I will do for them,
And not forsake them (Isaiah 42:16, NKJV*).*

Let the sins that have hindered you melt away like the winter snow, and allow his renewing strength to overwhelm your soul. Breathe in this fresh start. Today is a new day, full of promise and life. Receive the reward of salvation as a gift.

MAY 13

APPLICATION ACCEPTED

Applications are essential for gleaning the promising applicants from the inadequate. Fill out this form, and find out if you're approved for a home loan, for college admittance, for a credit card. We put our best qualities on paper, tweak our weaknesses, and hope for approval. But rejection is always a possibility.

With God, however, our acceptance has already been promised. We must only appeal to his son Jesus, who steps in on our behalf and petitions for our approval. There is no credit flaw, no failing grade, and no past default that his death on the cross doesn't redeem completely. Because we are covered with his loving forgiveness, there is no flaw in us. We are accepted by God as part of his family and redeemed by his grace for his eternal kingdom.

> *Long ago, even before he made the world, God chose us to be his very own through what Christ would do for us; he decided then to make us holy in his eyes, without a single fault—we who stand before him covered with his love (Ephesians 1:4, TLB).*

Can you believe your acceptance? Stand on the promise that there is nothing in your history—no past or present sin—that can separate you from his love. Cast everything upon him and have faith; you are wholly accepted and abundantly loved!

LOVE LIKE HE DOES

God's greatest commandments are to love him and to love one another. Loving him may come easy; after all, he is patient and loving himself. But the second part of his command can be difficult because it means loving intrusive neighbors at the backyard barbecue, offensive cousins at Christmas dinner, rude cashiers at the grocery store check-out, and insufferable guests who have stayed one night too many in the guestroom.

Loving one another is only possible when we love like him. When we love out of our humanity, sin gets in the way. Obeying the command to love begins with *his* love. When we realize how great his love is for us—how undeserved, unending, and unconditional—we are humbled because we didn't earn it. But he gives it anyway, freely and abundantly, and this spurs us on to love others.

We love because he first loved us (1 John 4:19, ESV).

We represent Jesus Christ to the world through love. If we know how high and wide and deep and long his love is for us, then we have no choice but to pour out that love on others. The intrusive becomes welcome, the offensive becomes peaceful, rudeness gives way to grace, and the insufferable is overshadowed by the cross and all that Jesus suffered there.

UNEXPECTED GENEROSITY

You pull up to the drive-through, place an order for the coffee that will help start your day, and hear the cashier's words, "Your order was paid for by the car in front of you." This unexpected generosity gives birth to humbling gratitude, and the day is now overcome with God's presence. A stranger may have been the instrument of kind provision, but the inspiration is unmistakable.

God is the author of generosity, providing us with all we need. Look at all he gave to Adam and Eve, and how little he asked for in return! They walked in his presence daily, enjoying authentic relationship with their Father. *Just don't eat the fruit from that tree or you will die.* Even when they ate it, God provided atonement for them.

> *Because of our faith, Chri st has brought us into this place of undeserved privilege where we now stand, and we confidently and joyfully look forward to sharing God's glory (Romans 5:2,* NLT*).*

We, like Adam and Eve, have sinned and deserve death. But Christ is our substantial provision! As if eternity in his kingdom weren't enough, he blesses us each and every day, whether we acknowledge it or not. Some things, like free coffee at the drive-through, are small provisions. Others are subtle or unseen altogether. But he is working his love out in generous portions for you, his beloved!

A STRONG, GRACEFUL OAK

How many thoughts does the human brain conceive in an hour? In a day? In a lifetime? How many of those thoughts are about God: who he is and what he has done for his children? Imagine your own thoughts about life—grocery lists, dentist appointments, song lyrics, lost keys—and your thoughts about God—his majesty, holiness, comfort, creativity—weighed against each other on a scale. Likely, it would tip in favor of the many details of human existence.

These temporary details overshadow the one comfort and promise we can rely on: the gospel of Jesus' birth, death, resurrection, and ascension for our eternal salvation. Wipe every other thought away and we are left with this truth. For those burdened by their sin it is of great comfort! Jesus came to give us new life!

> *To all who mourn… he will give: beauty for ashes; joy instead of mourning; praise instead of heaviness. For God has planted them like strong and graceful oaks for his own glory (Isaiah 61:3, TLB).*

You are not a weak sapling, limited by inadequate light and meager nourishment. You are a strong and graceful oak, soaring and resilient for the glory of God. Ashes and mourning and heavy burdens are relieved. The scales tip to this one weighty thought: you are his. Let your thoughts stretch above the canopy of everyday human details to bask in this joy: he has given you everything you need in Jesus.

MAY 17

ASSURANCE OF ETERNITY

In a matter of days, everything was destroyed. First his 11,000 livestock and servants were stolen, burned, or killed. Then his ten children all died at once. To make matters worse, this unfortunate man's skin was plagued with painful sores, which he scraped with a piece of broken pottery.

How could anyone endure such tragedy? To be fair, Job mourns, and laments, and weeps. He is confused, hopeless, and weak. On top of feeling cursed and desperate, he is taunted by his friends and wife: "Give up on God; he has given up on you! Stop waiting on God to redeem you; he has obviously forgotten you!"

Job's faith has been weakened by the test, but he clutches desperately to the one promise that can sustain him: no matter what happens to Job in his earth-bound life, nothing can take away the joy he will share with God in his eternal life.

> *"I know that my Redeemer lives,*
> *and he will stand upon the earth at last.*
> *And after my body has decayed,*
> *yet in my body I will see God! I will see him for myself.*
> *Yes, I will see him with my own eyes.*
> *I am overwhelmed at the thought!"* (Job 19:25-27, NLT)

Everything on earth is a fleeting treasure, a momentary comfort that can be lost in a flash. But the assurance of your eternal place in his kingdom, if you have submitted your life to Jesus Christ, is indestructible.

SAFETY GUARANTEED

Huddled in the basement of the museum, visitors waited for the hurricane to pass. Children cried or slept, parents' expressions were tight and anxious. Museum staff held walkie-talkies and flashlights, beams bouncing nervously. Sirens wailed, winds howled, and the depths of the shelter shook as the mighty storm raged outside.

Even with modern engineering advancements implemented, those sheltered from the storm were worried. There was no guarantee of safety. Could we expect the huddled crowds to be singing for joy? Rejoicing in their place of refuge? If they were aware of the one who has promised to always protect, then their praises would echo off of the shelter walls!

In the shadow of God's protection we can be glad. He is the only one able to guarantee our safety! His protection spreads over us, stronger than any bomb shelter or apocalyptic bunker we could engineer.

He will keep you from every form of evil or calamity
as he continually watches over you.
You will be guarded by God himself.
You will be safe when you leave your home
and safely you will return. He will protect you now,
and he'll protect you forevermore! (Psalm 121:7-8, TPT*).*

Can you relate to this need for protection today? Imagine delighting through the storm, singing while the structures come crashing down, knowing all the while that you are standing under the mighty hand of God.

MAY 19

CHOOSING COMPASSION

Consider the Israelites wandering in the desert: God had rescued them out of bondage and goes before them in a pillar of fire, providing for their every need and protecting them. What do they offer to him? Complaints.

Listen to the psalms of David—the man after God's own heart—as he lays his burdens at the feet of God, praising his majesty and might. But what does David do when he wants what he cannot have? Steals, murders, and lies.

Paul, who gave his life to preach the gospel he loved to people near and far, shares the astounding gift of God's grace to Jews and Gentiles alike. But who was he before his conversion? A hateful, persecuting murderer of Christians.

The Lord is compassionate and gracious,
Slow to anger and abounding in lovingkindness
(Psalm 103:8, NASB).

God loves his children regardless of their sin, their past, and their failings. We aren't dealt with as we deserve; rather, according to his great love for us. Can we say the same about how we treat those around us? Are we compassionate, slow to anger, and full of love? Or are we offended, impatient, and aggravated?

COME AWAY

Some say that romance is dead. It's not for God: the lover of our souls. He desires nothing more than time with his creation! It can be a little uncomfortable to have his gaze so intently upon us though. We're nothing special, after all! Not beauty queens, academic scholars, or athletic prodigies of any kind. We might not be musical, or crafty, or organized. Our house might be a mess, and we could probably use a manicure.

Do you feel a bit squeamish under such an adoring gaze? There is good news for you! You are, in fact, his beautiful one! And he does, indeed, want to bring you out of the cold winter. He's finished the watering season and it is finally—*finally*—time to rejoice in the season of renewal.

My beloved speaks and says to me:
"Arise, my love, my beautiful one,
and come away,
for behold, the winter is past;
the rain is over and gone.
The flowers appear on the earth,
the time of singing
has come" (Song of Solomon 2:10-12, ESV).

Why do you feel uncomfortable under the gaze of the one who loves you more than anyone else ever could? The time has come. He is calling you, regardless of how unworthy you may think you are. Will you arise and come away with your beloved? He is waiting for you!

MAY 21

NEVER-ENDING JOY

Consider for a moment the most joyous time of your walk with Christ. Imagine the delight of that season, the lightness and pleasure in your heart. Rest in the memory for a minute, and let the emotions come back to you. Is the joy returning? Do you feel it? Now, hear this truth: The way you felt about God at the highest, most joyful, amazing, glorious moment is how he feels about you *at all times!*

What a glorious blessing! Our joy is an overflow of his heart's joy toward us; it is just one of the many blessings God showers over us. When we realize how good he is, and that he has granted us everything we need for salvation through Jesus, we can rejoice!

My heart rejoices in the LORD!
The Lord has made me strong.
Now I have an answer for my enemies;
I rejoice because you rescued me.
No one is holy like the LORD!
There is no one besides you;
there is no Rock like our God (1 Samuel 2:1,2 NLT).

The season of your greatest rejoicing can be now, when you consider the strength he provides, the suffering from which you have been rescued, and the rock that is our God. His blessings don't depend on our feeling joyous; we experience joy because we realize God's gracious and loving blessings. Lift your praises to him and let your song be never-ending.

WAITING FOR DAWN

The sin and sadness of life can make it seem like an endless night, where we are continually waiting for the dawn of Christ's return. In the darkest of nights, it doesn't always help to know that he will return *someday*, because *this day* is full of despair.

To you, his beloved daughter, he gives comfort. Don't lose heart. He is coming for you! It can be hard, because he seems to be taking a long time, but he is preparing a place for you. You are not forgotten in this long night; your pain is familiar to him. Keep your eyes fixed on him! Soon you will hear his voice! He is also longing for that moment.

The ransomed of the LORD shall return,
and come to Zion with singing;
everlasting joy shall be upon their heads;
they shall obtain joy and gladness,
and sorrow and sighing shall flee away (Isaiah 35:10, NRSV).

We live for the promise of his return. This promise overcomes our pain, our longing, our desperation, and our limits. All things become bearable and light under the assurance of seeing Jesus, embracing him, and gazing on his beauty! We will be made into a pure and spotless bride. There is nothing more for us but to marvel at him. Glorify him. Believe him. Love him. Thank him.

MAY 23

EMBRACING WEAKNESS

Do you ever find yourself suddenly aware of your own glaring weaknesses? Aware that, if left up to your own good works, you wouldn't stand a chance of attaining salvation? We should find great comfort in the fact that we are nothing without salvation in Christ Jesus.

Thankfully, God made a way for us to be united with him, despite impatience, selfishness, anger, and pride. God deeply cares for us and patiently sustains us with steady, faithful, and adoring love. Amazingly, his love even goes beyond this to *embrace* and *transform* our weakness when we yield it to him. Weakness isn't something to be feared or hidden; weakness submitted to God allows the power of Christ to work in and through us.

When we know our weakness, we are more aware of our need for his strength. When we put ourselves in a position of humility and ask him to be strong where we are weak, he is delighted to help. You don't have to ask a knight in shining armor twice to rescue his princess.

> *Humble yourselves in the sight of the Lord, and He will lift you up (James 4:10, NKJV).*

Prayerfully submit your weakness to God so that, through him, you can be strong. His transformative love is waiting to graciously restore you.

MAY 24

UNENDING CHORUS

Some days begin with praises on our lips and a song to God in our hearts. Humility covers us like a velvet cloth, soothing and delicate and gentle. The truth of God plays on repeat: "God is good! God is good! I am free!" and the entire world's darkness cannot interrupt the chorus.

But other days begin by fumbling with the snooze button and forfeiting the chance to meet him in the quiet stillness. Pride, then, is a sneaky companion, pushing and bitter and ugly, and we wonder if we will ever delight with God again. We feel bound.

The ups and downs should be familiar by now, perhaps, but can we ever become accustomed to the holy living side-by-side with our flesh? One glorious day, flesh will give way to freedom, and there will be no side-by-side. Only the holy will remain. This leaves praise on our lips and a song in our hearts, the unending chorus of his goodness, the velvet covering as we sit before his heavenly throne.

Creation itself will be set free from its bondage to corruption and obtain the freedom of the glory of the children of God (Romans 8:21, ESV).

Do you know how much God wants you to rest in his presence? He is waiting and faithful and tender. When you spend time with him, there is no need to hide. You can be exactly who you are. There is freedom in his presence.

MAY 25

A WORTHY FRIEND

God created you for relationship with him just as he created Adam and Eve. He delights in your voice, your laughter, and your ideas. He longs to fellowship with you just as he did with his first son and daughter.

The friendship God offers to us is a gift of immeasurable worth. There is no one like him; indeed, there is none as worthy of our fellowship than God Almighty, our Maker and Redeemer. Train your heart to run first to him with your pain, joy, frustration, and excitement. His friendship will never let you down!

Let all that I am praise the LORD;
may I never forget the good things he does for me.
He forgives all my sins
and heals all my diseases.
He redeems me from death
and crowns me with love and tender mercies.
He fills my life with good things.
My youth is renewed like the eagle's! (Psalm 103:2-5, NLT)

When life gets difficult, do you run to him with your frustrations? When you're overwhelmed with sadness or grief, do you carry your pain to him? In the heat of anger or frustration, do you call on him for freedom? He is a friend that offers all of this to us—and more—in mercy and love. He is worthy of your friendship.

A MIGHTY KING?

When Jesus, the long awaited Messiah, revealed his deity to his family, his disciples, and the crowds, they were expecting a mighty king who would deliver them from their oppressors and establish his everlasting kingdom. What they got was a humble servant who dined with tax collectors and whose feet were cleansed by the tears of a prostitute. Jesus wasn't exactly what they thought he would be.

He was better! He came to bring salvation to those who were drowning in a sea of sin and sickness; those who were cast out and in need of holy redemption; those whom the religious leaders had deemed unworthy but whose hearts longed for true restoration. He came to redeem his people, but not in the way they expected.

"The Spirit of the Lord is upon me,
because he has anointed me
to proclaim good news to the poor.
He has sent me to proclaim liberty to the captives
and recovering of sight to the blind,
to set at liberty those who are oppressed,
to proclaim the year of the Lord's favor"(Luke 4:18-19, ESV).

Jesus delivers you from the bonds of sin and oppression through his death and resurrection and through your repentance from sin by faith. The Spirit of the Lord is upon you and he has anointed you! Proclaim this good news today; you have been set free!

MAY 27

ALWAYS THERE

From famous songs to television commercials to close friends, there's a promise that is often made and rarely kept. *I'm here for you; you can always count on me.* Most of us have been promised this sometime in our life, and most, if not all, have felt that sting of rejection or disappointment when things didn't quite turn out that way.

In the midst of our trying circumstances, we call out to the people who promised to always be there, but they don't answer. They don't even call us back. Even the best friend, the closest sister, the doting parent will fail in their ability to be there for you.

But there is someone who you *can* always count on. You can tell him everything. He *hears* you. He'll wrap his arms around you, stroke your hair, and tell you everything is going to be all right. He is completely trustworthy.

God's way is perfect.
All the Lord's promises prove true.
He is a shield for all who look to him for protection.
For who is God except the Lord?
Who but our God is a solid rock? (Psalm 18:30-31 NLT)

Have you been disappointed or hurt by someone you love? Trust in the one who is dependable. God will always be there for you.

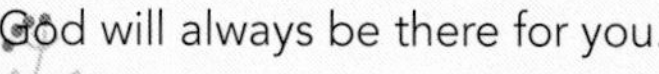

OVERWHELMING DEVOTION

God in his great power and faithfulness never fails us, never gives up on us, and will never leave us alone, out on a limb, to fend for ourselves. His love for us remains—regardless of our circumstances or our weaknesses—strong and immovable. His devotion to his children exceeds that of all parents, whose love for their children seems unmatched, but is only human. Not only does God match our love, he surpasses it. He is without limits, and nothing can ever change God's devotion.

This truth is overwhelmingly satisfying; when such devotion has been proven, what else could attract our gaze? Where else could our eyes find such beauty and purity as they do upon the face of Jesus? In awe, we recognize that his gaze is fixed right back at us, seeing us as a lovely and worthy prize. We can neither deserve this gaze nor escape it. We are flawed, but he is unwavering in his love for us.

This forever-song I sing of the gentle love of God overwhelming me!
Young and old alike will hear about
your faithful, steadfast love—never failing!
Here's my chorus: "Your mercy grows through the ages.
Your faithfulness is firm, rising up to the skies"
(Psalm 89:1-2, TPT).

Do you know that the Father is wholly devoted to you? His great love for you is yours to enjoy forever.

MAY 29

TRUE SATISFACTION

Stress threatens to get the better of us, and sometimes we just want to hide. Remembering that secret bar of chocolate in the pantry, we may scurry off to do just that: bury ourselves away with the temporary but sweet comfort that helps the world slow down, if only for a moment.

The same instinct can arise with God. We get overwhelmed by his ministry or overdue for his forgiveness or out of touch with his Word and lose track of who he is. Instead of running toward him, we hide from him and look for other ways to meet our needs. We cannot hide from him, and in love he calls out to us.

O my dove, in the clefts of the rock,
in the crannies of the cliff,
let me see your face,
let me hear your voice,
for your voice is sweet,
and your face is lovely (Song of Solomon 2:14, ESV*).*

You cannot outrun his love for you, nor should you try. Instead, leave the false safety of the clefts and crannies and pantries with hidden chocolate. Feel the pleasure of his friendship: this God who wants to hear your voice and see your face because he finds them sweet and lovely. Is there anyone else who can satisfy you so perfectly?

WANDERING IN THE COURTYARD

Once upon a time, a courtyard in a faraway land overflowed with lost children. They were all very dirty, dressed in threadbare garments, and deeply hungry. Some children had gaping wounds, others were bruised or limping. A man walked among them, gently tending to their needs.

Next to the courtyard was a majestic castle with bright flags and high winding turrets. The doors of the castle were wide open, and inside was a banquet with delicious food, warm fires, and robes of velvet. A king sat inside, surrounded by his children who were clean, fed, and smiling.

Two children approached the doorway, smelling the food and feeling the warmth from the castle. The man in the courtyard took their hands and asked if they would like to join the king as his children. One leaped for joy, and, not waiting another second, ran into the castle. The other held back, looked down at her filthy rags, and shook her head. She wandered back amongst the other children.

When the right time came, God sent his Son, born of a woman, subject to the law. God sent him to buy freedom for us who were slaves to the law, so that he could adopt us as his very own children (Galatians 4:4-5, NLT).

Daughter, are you wandering in the courtyard? Why do you believe that your sins make you unworthy of God's banquet? You have been bought at a high price and are adopted into the family of God.

SOUND OF A WHISPER

We often want, more than anything, to "go the distance" for God. Our deepest desire is to sacrifice for him no matter the cost. But what we don't always realize is that past the sacrifice, past the actions, and past the gifts, God really just wants our hearts.

We strain to hear from God, and we expect his answer in a thunderous clap; we search for him in a firestorm. But when we are at the end of ourselves, down on our knees before him, then he will speak in that still, small voice that we have to be broken and humbled to hear.

> *"A great and strong wind tore the mountains and broke in pieces the rocks before the Lord, but the Lord was not in the wind. And after the wind an earthquake, but the Lord was not in the earthquake. And after the earthquake a fire, but the Lord was not in the fire. And after the fire the sound of a low whisper" (1 Kings 19:11-12, ESV).*

We know the character of God, but we still look for him to act outside of it on a daily basis. We know that he is after our hearts, but we seek to give him more because we fear, deep down, that our hearts won't be enough. God speaks in a whisper because he wants to reveal to us that he isn't about the show. He just wants us to love him.

JUNE

God will generously provide all you need. Then you will always have everything you need and plenty left over to share with others.

2 Corinthians 9:8 NLT

JUNE 1

LIFTING THE VEIL

Even when we accept Christ as our Savior, there is often a wall that we put up in our hearts. We strive to love him with every fiber of our being, but there can be failure to give him all of us. It's as if the most human part of us feels that by maintaining that last bit of space, we protect ourselves and are free to be who we'd rather be.

True freedom is experienced when we give up, give in, and give ourselves over completely. He wants to take away that veil that prevents us from fully seeing all the beauty that he has in store for us.

> *Whenever anyone turns to the Lord, the veil is taken away. Now the Lord is the Spirit, and where the Spirit of the Lord is, there is freedom. And we all, who with unveiled faces contemplate the Lord's glory, are being transformed into his image with ever-increasing glory, which comes from the Lord, who is the Spirit (2 Corinthians 3:16-18,* NIV*).*

Pray that your veil will be lifted—that the last piece of you that may be resisting his Spirit will be given to him today. Experience the freedom that is his glory!

TRULY SPECIAL

We all want to believe that we are special. Most of us grow up being told that we are, and it feels good to believe it. But over time, we look around us and realize that, really, we are just like everyone else. Doubt begins to creep in, making us second guess ourselves and damaging our self-confidence.

Long before you were even a wisp in your mother's womb, you were set aside and marked as special. You were chosen to be God's special possession, and that's a pretty amazing thing.

> *You are a chosen people, a royal priesthood, a holy nation, God's special possession, that you may declare the praises of him who called you out of darkness into his wonderful light. Once you were not a people, but now you are the people of God; once you had not received mercy, but now you have received mercy (1 Peter 2:9-10, NIV).*

God sees you as special. Revel in that knowledge today. He is calling you out of the darkness of the ordinary, and bringing you into the light of the extraordinary. He picked you. He loves you. He wants you. Trust in that.

JUNE 3

HE UNDERSTANDS TEMPTATION

One of the most beautiful things about the God we serve is that he knows exactly what we are going through at any given time. How does he know? Because he has been there himself.

When Jesus came to earth in the form of a human, he was tempted by the same everyday things we are. Whether it's lust, unkind thoughts, unwarranted anger... you name it, he had to face it. Just like we do.

> *Since we have a great high priest, Jesus the Son of God, who has gone into heaven, let us hold on to the faith we have. For our high priest is able to understand our weaknesses. He was tempted in every way that we are, but he did not sin (Hebrews 4:14-15,* NCV*).*

You can bring your temptation and confessed sin to the Lord without fear; he knows exactly how you're feeling. He is not some far off God in the sky who cannot relate to you and your life. Pray for protection from temptation just as he did, and he will answer you!

REST SECURE

No matter where you are, God is there also. While there may be times when we ache to hide from him in our shame, he is a constant presence. The beautiful thing about his omnipresence is that we have a steady and consistent companion who is always ready to help in times of trouble.

We have no reason to fear the things that the world may throw our way. We've got the best protector of all at our side! Are you asking for his help in times of worry and woe, or are you turning inward to try to solve your problems?

I keep my eyes always on the Lord.
With him at my right hand, I will not be shaken.
Therefore my heart is glad and my tongue rejoices;
my body also will rest secure (Psalm 16:8-9, NIV).

Let God be your refuge. Nothing is too big or too small for him! Even in your darkest hours, you can know true joy because he is your guardian. Take your cares and distress, and cast them upon him, because he can handle it. Rest secure in him.

JUNE 5

A LIVING SACRIFICE

To live the life that we are supposed to as Christians, quite simply, is really hard. We are called to be a reflection of Jesus, and that can seem pretty unattainable.

Truly, it is, especially if we strive to do it on our own. We are only able to live as we should if we do it hand-in-hand with the Holy Spirit. It's in our nature to want to conform to the ways of this world. But we can fight against that temptation and win with God on our side.

> *Our faces, then, are not covered. We all show the Lord's glory, and we are being changed to be like him. This change in us brings ever greater glory, which comes from the Lord, who is the Spirit. (2 Corinthians 3:18, NCV).*

In what ways are you conforming to the ways of this world? Pray for protection from that today. Offer yourself to the Lord as a living sacrifice, and he will honor you for it!

KINDNESS DEFINED

Kindness. It's an attribute so important to God that he listed it among the fruit of the spirit (along with some other pretty good ones: love, joy, peace, patience, goodness, faithfulness, gentleness, and self-control). But what does it really mean? Is it just being friendly to others? Being nice?

True kindness is defined as being more than that. It's also being generous and considerate. It's a choice we make each day. We choose to be generous with our time and with our funds. We opt to consider others' feelings before our own. The Bible talks about kindness quite a lot. Even Job, in his misery, recognized how generous and considerate the Lord was of him. When wave after wave of heartbreak took over Job, he still saw God's kindness.

You gave me life and showed me kindness,
and in your providence watched over my spirit
(Job 10:12, NIV).

Are you choosing kindness in your day-to-day life? Are you going beyond just being friendly, and being generous? Look for ways in which you can be considerate of others today. Pray that God will open your eyes to the needs of others and show you ways to be compassionate.

JUNE 7

FOREVER FASHION

Fashion comes and goes. It can be really fun to see what's new in stores each season, finding pieces that update our look and wardrobe. There's nothing quite like the feeling of finding an item that makes us feel great every time we put it on—that one thing we knew was *it* when we saw it in the store.

Fashion is fun, but God calls us to clothe ourselves in something even better than the latest look off the runway. He wants us to get dressed each day in something that will make us feel even better than our favorite sweater or a great pair of heels. We are to be clothed in beautiful character traits that emulate Jesus Christ.

> *As God's chosen people, holy and dearly loved, clothe yourselves with compassion, kindness, humility, gentleness and patience (Colossians 3:12,* NIV*).*

What are you wearing today? Are you all dressed up in compassion? Have you covered yourself with a dose of humility? Is gentleness draped around you, and patience your perfume? Trends in fashion may come and go, but kindness never goes out of style. Wear it proudly!

JUNE 8

GLORY ORIGIN

When we achieve great things, it can become easy to forget where our successes come from. *I worked so hard*, we tell ourselves. *I did so much to earn this!* There is nothing wrong with climbing the ladder of success, whatever that is to you, but when we neglect to give the honor to God for all of our achievements, we lose sight of the victory itself.

Instead, we should do it all for the glory of God. He is the one who gives us all that we have. He wants us to be successful in our endeavors, but he also wants us to remember from where that success came from. We need to remember to humble ourselves in the midst of our triumphs.

In your glory and grandeur go forth in victory!
Through your faithfulness and meekness
the cause of truth and justice will stand.
Awe-inspiring miracles are accomplished by your power,
leaving everyone dazed and astonished! (Psalm 45:4, TPT)

Have you thanked the Lord for what you've achieved? While you slay those dragons, take some time to praise God. Go ahead and go for the gold, but give the glory to him, remaining humble all the while.

JUNE 9

PROCLAIMING FAITH

Have you ever been afraid of what others will think of you when they learn that you are a Christian? Do you ever worry that people may assume you are some sort of weirdo if you proclaim your faith? It can be hard enough to fit in without giving society another reason to shun you.

Be assured, there is no reason to be afraid! God has given us his Holy Spirit to guide us through tough conversations. Be bashful no more—he has equipped you with all the talent you need to share his love with those around you. There will be some who will laugh, and there will be some who will scorn you for your beliefs. The Lord himself tells us through his Word that we have nothing to fear.

May he give you the power to accomplish all the good things your faith prompts you to do (2 Thessalonians 1:11, NLT).

Shake off your timidity! Picture yourself shedding it like a winter coat in the warmth of spring. Be prepared to share your faith without fear! God has sent his Holy Spirit to give you power when you lack it. Take advantage of it!

GOOD COMPANY

When we spend a great deal of time with people, we begin to act as they do. We start to emulate their actions, and copy their behavior. When we choose our friends, we need to choose wisely.

Are we surrounding ourselves with those who follow the example Christ set for us? Or is our crowd one that does whatever the flesh desires? If someone who didn't know our hearts took a look at our lives, would they see Jesus in it?

> *Join together in following my example, brothers and sisters, and just as you have us as a model, keep your eyes on those who live as we do. For, as I have often told you before and now tell you again even with tears, many live as enemies of the cross of Christ. Their destiny is destruction, their god is their stomach, and their glory is in their shame. Their mind is set on earthly things. But our citizenship is in heaven. And we eagerly await a Savior from there, the Lord Jesus Christ (Philippians 3:17-20, NIV).*

Seek friends who are determined to live as Christians are called to do. Together, you can set your eyes on the prize of an eternal life in heaven.

JUNE 11

MELODY OF WORSHIP

Have you ever felt the song of your heart praising the Lord? No words may come, no verses, no chorus, and yet your very being feels as though it may burst from the music inside you. You are not alone! Even the very heavens praise him in this way!

The Bible tells us that without words, and without even the slightest sound, the skies burst forth in a song of praise for the glory of God. Isn't that an amazing picture? Can't you just envision an orchestra above you?

God's splendor is a tale that is told;
his testament is written in the stars.
Space itself speaks his story every day
through the marvels of the heavens.
His truth is on tour in a starry-vault of the sky,
showing his skill in creation's craftsmanship.
Every day gushes out its message to the next,
night with night whispering its knowledge to all.
Without a sound, without a word,
without a voice being heard,
Yet all the world can see its story.
Everywhere its gospel is clearly read so all may know
(Psalm 19:1-4, TPT).

Break forth into your song! Allow your heart to feel the words, even if you cannot fully form them. Give God all your praises today. He is so deserving of them! Let your heart be a celebration of your love for Jesus Christ. Give in to the melody of worship inside you.

TOP PRIORITY

It's so easy to fall prey to the wants and desires of the world. There's the latest this, and the coolest that, and we have a hunger to own it all. We see our neighbor with the newest piece of technology, and suddenly ours seems out of date. Our friend shows up for coffee with a fancy necklace, recently purchased from a high-end store, and we ache to add it to our collection.

There's nothing inherently wrong with shopping, and we're not sinning simply by making an acquisition. It's more about the priority we give our purchases than the purchases themselves. It's about the heart.

> *Do not love the world or anything in the world. If anyone loves the world, love for the Father is not in them. For everything in the world—the lust of the flesh, the lust of the eyes, and the pride of life—comes not from the Father but from the world (1 John 2:15-16,* NIV*).*

What are you putting first in your life? Are you coveting all that the world has to offer, or is the ache in your heart a yearning for Jesus' presence? Pray for protection from the desires of the world today.

JUNE 13

PRAISE THROUGH CIRCUMSTANCE

When life is good, it is easy to praise God. *My life is full of blessings,* we think to ourselves. *He is so good to me!* But what happens when life is hard? Do we continue to give him the glory when we're thrown curveball after curveball?

Regardless of our circumstance, whatever our situation, we need to continue to give him the praises he so richly deserves. A life lived alongside Christ doesn't mean it will be one free of pain, of discomfort, of tough times. But it does mean that we can find contentment in it anyway because we have him in our lives to turn to.

> *I have learned to be content whatever the circumstances. I know what it is to be in need, and I know what it is to have plenty. I have learned the secret of being content in any and every situation, whether well fed or hungry, whether living in plenty or in want. I can do all this through him who gives me strength (Philippians 4:11-13,* NIV*).*

Pray for contentment today, whatever your circumstance. There is no crisis that the Lord is not willing to walk you through. You can do anything with him at your side!

JUNE 14

ALL OF YOU

The Pharisees were always trying to trip up Jesus. They wanted nothing more than to find fault with him—a reason to put him on trial or do away with him. So when they asked him which of all the commandments was the greatest, they were hoping that he would somehow fail to come up with the correct answer.

Instead, as usual, he got it right. And, oh! How right it was. When we love the Lord our God with all our hearts, everything else falls into place. The other commandments are easy to follow! We cannot truly love him and continue to fall short in other areas.

> *One of them, an expert in the law, tested him with this question: "Teacher, which is the greatest commandment in the Law?"*
> *Jesus replied: "'Love the Lord your God with all your heart and with all your soul and with all your mind.' This is the first and greatest commandment"* (Matthew 22:34-38, NIV).

Have you given all of yourself to him? Do you love the Lord your God with *all* of your heart, *all* of your soul, and *all* of your mind? Let the last of your walls crumble, and give him all of you today!

JUNE 15

THE SON BEFORE THE SUN

When do you find time to pray? Even if we are intentional and passionate about prayer, the everyday activities in our life will almost always take priority over time with God. It is often said that prayer can happen at any time, and of course it does, but is there value in setting aside a specific time to communicate with the Lord?

Did you ever realize that the notion of *quiet times* comes from the example set by Jesus? We see in the Bible that Jesus would get up before daylight and pray in a solitary place. We are not often told what Jesus prayed about. It's not the content that matters; it's the willingness to maintain our relationship with the Father and seek his will. What better time to do this than at the beginning of our day?

> *Now in the morning, having risen a long while before daylight, He went out and departed to a solitary place; and there He prayed (Mark 1:35,* NKJV*).*

Instead of trying to fit prayer into your busy day, pray before it gets busy, so that you can cope with the pressures of life. Are you able to give God some time in the early morning? Can you find a solitary place to hear from him? Be like Jesus and find the time and space to wait upon the Father.

HELP NEEDED

Help! We don't often verbalize this word, but we certainly internalize it, probably more often than we realize. What do you do in times of need? Who do you rely on to get you through a tough situation?

Jesus asked the Father to give us a helper, one that would always be with us, and one that speaks truth. This is the Holy Spirit, and this is his role in our lives. Jesus promised that the Spirit of truth would abide in us because we have received him through our belief in him.

> *"I will ask the Father, and He will give you another Helper, that He may be with you forever; that is the Spirit of truth, whom the world cannot receive, because it does not see Him or know Him, but you know Him because He abides with you and will be in you"* (John 14:16-17, NASB).

Are you confronting a difficult situation today? Are you struggling to be obedient to the Lord? Are you anxious about anything? The world may think it has answers, but it does not know the Spirit. The Spirit is present in you at all times and will speak the truth. So ask for his help today and be willing to receive it!

JUNE 17

A LIGHT TO THE END

It was always part of God's plan to bring salvation to his entire creation. We know the people of Israel are the chosen ones through whom God brought salvation, but we need to remember that God wanted his message to go to the ends of the earth.

Jesus didn't confine his ministry to the Jewish people and believers of his day. He extended his ministry to the Gentiles and everyone "outside" the law of the Scribes and the Pharisees.

Indeed He says,
"It is too small a thing that You should be My Servant
To raise up the tribes of Jacob,
And to restore the preserved ones of Israel;
I will also give You as a light to the Gentiles,
That You should be My salvation to the ends of the earth"
(Isaiah 49:6, NKJV).

God doesn't want us to keep him to ourselves. He wants us to be a light that shines for all to see so that salvation can reach the ends of the earth. Are you willing to be that light for Christ today?

MAKE YOUR COMPLAINT

Life's not fair. Think of games, or races, or even schooling. Someone always comes out on top, and there are always losers. We can influence some outcomes, but there are many things that are outside of our control. We cannot guarantee that we will be protected from the troubles of this life.

So what do we do when we feel like complaining about our misfortunes? We often feel like we have no right to complain to God—we are told to be thankful in all things, right? Well, yes, but God can handle your complaints and your cry for answers, just as David asks him to in this Psalm.

I cry out to the Lord with my voice;
With my voice to the Lord I make my supplication.
I pour out my complaint before Him;
I declare before Him my trouble (Psalm 142:1-2, NKJV).

It can be healthy to discuss your troubles with God. Using your voice is important to revealing what is going on in your heart. Do you feel like making your complaints known today? Instead of voicing them to others, pour them out before the Lord. He is understanding and gracious, and he promises to be with you in all things.

JUNE 19

UNFAILING GOODNESS

Do you remember the first thing that you failed at? Maybe it was a test at school, a diet, a job interview, or even a relationship. Failure is difficult to admit, especially in a culture that values outward success and appearance. We often hear it said that success comes from many failures, but we only really hear that from successful people!

When Joshua was "advanced in years," he reminded the Israelites of all that God had done for them. Though they had been unfaithful to God many times, God remained faithful, and they became a great nation that none could withstand.

> *"I am about to go the way of all the earth, and you know in your hearts and souls, all of you, that not one thing has failed of all the good things that the LORD your God promised concerning you; all have come to pass for you, not one of them has failed"* (Joshua 23:14, NRSV).

God had a plan and a purpose for the nation of Israel, and through his power and mercy he ensured that these plans succeeded. In the same way, God has a purpose for your life, and while you may fail, he will not. Take the opportunity today to submit your heart to his will. Know that not one good thing that God has planned for you will fail.

ORDERED STEPS

If you've ever taken the hand of a toddler, you'll know that they are relying on you for their balance. If they stumble, you can easily steady them. This simple act of holding a hand means that you and the child have confidence that they won't fall flat on their face!

In the same way, when we commit our way to God, we are essentially placing our hand in his. He delights in the fact that we are walking with him. Even in the times when we stumble, he will steady our path and give us the confidence to keep walking.

I will instruct you in the way you should go;
I will counsel you with my loving eye on you (Psalm 32:8, NIV).

Do you feel like you have stumbled lately, or are unsure of your walk with God? Be confident that the Lord delights in your commitment to him. Accept his hand, continue to walk, and trust him to keep you from falling.

JUNE 21

HONOR YOUR PARENTS

Have you ever felt like your parents didn't really know what they were doing when they were raising you? Well, of course they didn't—it's something they had to learn every step of the way!

Not all of us had a great childhood, and many of us can hold on to resentment about the way we were raised. However, God gave the commandment to his people to honor their father and mother, whether they deserved it or not.

> *"Honor your father and your mother, as the LORD your God has commanded you, that your days may be long, and that it may be well with you in the land which the LORD your God is giving you"* (Deuteronomy 5:16, NKJV).

How can you honor your father or mother today? Whether your parents are around or not, you can be thankful for the good things they have given you, and you can also be gracious about their faults. Remember that God wants to bring restoration to relationships. Allow him to provide you with a gracious and loving heart toward your parents, today.

ETERNAL FOUNTAINS

We take it for granted that when we turn on a faucet, water will come out. If we need something to drink, we can quench our thirst pretty easily. In Jesus' day, however, people (usually women) had to get their water from the well, often situated quite a walk away from their homes. It was a necessary daily task that provided for the family's needs.

Imagine then, being offered water that would last forever. This is what Jesus offered the woman at the well. She would never have to make this trip again in the heat of the day. She wanted this answer to her need. Jesus compared her desire with a spiritual desire: just as the well was a source for physical life, he was the source for eternal life.

> *"Whoever drinks of the water that I shall give him will never thirst. But the water that I shall give him will become in him a fountain of water springing up into everlasting life" (John 4:14,* NKJV*).*

You have received Jesus as the source for your life. Not only does Jesus say that he will provide you with everlasting water, but he says that this water will be like a fountain, springing up. Are you thankful for the eternal life that Jesus has placed within you? Remember to draw from him as your source of life today.

JUNE 23

DIVINE PROMISES

When Adam and Eve were caught in their sin, they were ashamed. Instead of repenting, they tried to protect themselves by placing the blame somewhere else. It was the woman's fault, wasn't it? Or was it the snake's fault? God punished all of them; the truth is that they were each responsible for their own decision.

Lies have been around ever since the Garden of Eden. We don't respond much differently than Adam and Eve did when we try to hide our wrongdoing. We are quick to create excuses for ourselves; nobody likes to feel ashamed. Unfortunately, because we know that we stray from the truth at times, we are often uncertain of the truth in others. This is human nature. But it is not God's nature.

"God is not a man, that He should lie,
Nor a son of man, that he should repent.
Has he said, and will he not do?
Or has he spoken, and will he not make it good?"
(Numbers 23:19, NKJV)

God is fully divine; he cannot lie. What God has spoken is truth, so we can trust that his promises will endure. Do you sometimes doubt God's presence, or help, or goodness in your life? Take time to read his Word today and believe that these are his words of truth, and that they will prevail.

JUNE 24

CONFUSED?

Sometimes when we are seeking answers for a decision, we can receive so many "words" that we end up having more questions than when we started! Have you ever been prayed for and received words that seemed to contradict each other? Have you ever felt confused, either not understanding a word, or not knowing which word was truly from God?

The Scripture tells us that the church at Corinth was experiencing this difficulty. Having been filled with the Holy Spirit, the saints were so enthusiastic that all kinds of prophecies and revelations were being spoken. This lack of order became confusing for people, so Paul encouraged the saints to communicate their words responsibly.

> *God is not the author of confusion but of peace, as in all the churches of the saints (1 Corinthians 14:33, NKJV).*

God has chosen to speak through his people and that comes with a responsibility to declare God's words in a way that produces peace, not confusion. If you are experiencing confusion in your circumstances right now, pray that God gives you discernment of the truth. Read his Word and allow his peace to guide you in all things.

JUNE 25

STEP OUT IN FAITH

God doesn't often show us the entire plan when he calls us to do something. Joshua and the Israelites had to cross the Jordan River before they could enter the Promised Land. God told Joshua that he would part the waters for them. The priests, leading the way with the ark, walked into the water first. There stood the priests—partially immersed in water—waiting for God to do what he said he would. It must have taken great faith to stand in the water, waiting for the miracle to happen.

Sometimes God will have us walk right into a river before he parts the water because the work he can do in our hearts with a simple act of faith is well worth our fear.

> *Tell the priests who carry the ark of the covenant: "When you reach the edge of the Jordan's waters, go and stand in the river" (Joshua 3:7-8, NIV).*

If God were to show you the step-by-step plan, then faith wouldn't be necessary. God knows what your humanity can handle, and in light of that, he won't share with you what you don't need to know. God doesn't lie or change his mind, and he will not forget what he has told you. If you can trust him enough to step out into the water, he will do as he promised and you will walk forward on dry ground.

JUNE 26

THE WORD

We are met with a lot of opposition in our daily pursuit of Christ. We get sidetracked so easily with the things of this world, our own emotional struggles, and our war with sin. Without the truth of the living, active Word of God, we are defenseless to successfully live the Christian life.

The Word of God is our best defense against hopelessness, fear, and sin—and at the same time it's our best offensive weapon against temptation, lies, and the enemy of our souls.

How can a young man keep his way pure?
By guarding it according to your word.
With my whole heart I seek you;
let me not wander from your commandments!
I have stored up your word in my heart,
that I might not sin against you (Psalm 119:9-11, ESV).

Make a goal for yourself to memorize Scripture that will equip you for daily living. Paste verses in your calendar, hang them on your refrigerator, and frame them on your walls. The Word of God is the most useful, instructive, powerful book that you will ever get your hands on. Eat it, absorb it, know it, and live it.

JUNE 27

APPROVAL

What motivates you to be spiritual? Do you try to speak eloquently in church so that other people will be impressed by what you have to say, or do you speak out of sincere love for Christ and a desire to edify his body with truth? Do you raise your hands in worship so that other people around you will notice your connection with Christ, or do you worship because you are so overcome with love for your Savior?

Our words must be motivated out of love for God, or they mean nothing. Our praise must be born out of love for God, or it is just noise.

> *Am I now seeking the approval of man, or of God? Or am I trying to please man? If I were still trying to please man, I would not be a servant of Christ (Galatians 1:10,* ESV*).*

As you serve Christ and follow him, continually evaluate in your heart whether or not you are acting out of a desire to impress others or God. Paul is clear that those who are trying to please other people are not serving Christ. Keep your heart and your eyes fixed on God because he is the only one worthy of your praise.

JUNE 28

BUSYNESS

Our lives are so full that we often have difficulty finding time to spend with Jesus. We have so much that demands our attention, it can be hard to find time to consecrate a portion of our day to God.

God, who has existed for eternity, is not bound by time. Because he is outside of time, time does not limit him the way that it limits us. When we take even a few sacred minutes to spend in his presence in the midst of our busy day, he can meet us there and download deep truths to our hearts.

> *"Come away by yourselves to a secluded place and rest a while." (For there were many people coming and going, and they did not even have time to eat.) (Mark 6:31,* NASB*)*

In the days when you feel you don't even have time to eat, ask God to give you the grace to find a few moments to slip away alone in his presence. God will speak volumes to a heart that is open to his truth—even over the hustle and bustle of your busiest days.

JUNE 29

LIVING WORD

Have you ever noticed God speaking to you in themes? We all go through different seasons in life, and God speaks to our hearts accordingly. Some of us may be going through a season of learning to wait, while another is learning how to step out in faith. But the beautiful thing about God is that he is big enough to speak to all of us—in our different places, with our different hearts—at the same time, with the same words.

God's Word is alive and active. It can deliver truth to the heart of each unique person. Two people can get something completely different from the same passage of Scripture because of what God has been doing in each of their hearts separately. Through the body of Christ, we can come together and share what God is teaching us—multiplying our individual growth as we encourage one another.

> *The word of God is living and active and sharper than any two-edged sword, and piercing as far as the division of soul and spirit, of both joints and marrow, and able to judge the thoughts and intentions of the heart (Hebrews 4:12, NASB).*

Never doubt the power of what you hold in your hands when you read the Word of God. Your Creator knows you so intimately because he is the one who handcrafted your soul—and he cares about you enough to speak directly to your heart through his living Word.

FOR SUCH A TIME AS THIS

Sometimes it can be hard to be happy where you are. Looking ahead gives us something to hope for, and it can be easy to wish yourself away from the place God has you right now.

Because God designed us to long for heaven, we have an innate tendency to look ahead. But how do we find satisfaction in where God has us right now without always running ahead to the next thing? How do we live our lives to the fullest right where we are when we have a deep longing to be elsewhere?

When Esther found out the king's plans to destroy the Jews, she must have thought that God made a mistake in having her marry him. She probably wished that someone else had been chosen to be queen. But God chose her.

> *"If you keep quiet at a time like this, deliverance and relief for the Jews will arise from some other place, but you and your relatives will die. Who knows if perhaps you were made queen for just such a time as this?"* (Esther 4:14, NLT)

You may feel like a situation in your life is impossible. You may wish you were somewhere else, or that someone else had been given your set of circumstances. But God chose you. God makes no mistakes. He chose you to be right where you are to accomplish the work he has for you there. You were chosen for such a time as this.

His teachings make us joyful
and radiate his light;
his precepts are so pure!
His commands, how they challenge us
to keep close to his heart!
The revelation-light of his Word
makes my spirit shine radiant.

Psalm 19:8 TPT

UNCOMPLICATED FREEDOM

We over-complicate freedom in the Christian life. Through our legalisms, we try to find a way to humanize the redeeming work of the cross because we simply can't wrap our minds around the supernatural character of God.

It can be hard to understand the complete grace offered at Calvary because we are incapable of giving that kind of grace. But when God says that he has forgotten our sin, and that he has made us new, he really means it. God is love, and love keeps no record of wrongs. Nothing can keep us from his love. Salvation tore the veil that separated us from the holiness of God. That complete work cannot be diminished or erased by anything we do.

I have swept away your offenses like a cloud,
your sins like the morning mist.
Return to me,
for I have redeemed you (Isaiah 44:22, NIV).

Freedom is truly that simple. The beauty of the Gospel can be summed up in this single concept—grace, though undeserved, given without restraint. Accept it today. Walk in complete grace without question.

JULY 2

SAND CASTLES

Have you ever been sitting on a beach and watched a little child work tirelessly on an elaborate sand castle? They spend hours perfecting their creation, thoughtfully forming each section, often stepping back to admire their work. But these little children are unaware of the patterns of ocean waves and don't realize that as the day passes, their masterpieces will eventually be swept away by the swelling tide. All that work, all that concentration, all that pride, gone as the water erases the shore.

What proverbial castles are we building in our lives that could, at any moment, be simply erased? We've got to buy into the bigger vision. We must know what can last and what won't. There are temporary kingdoms and a kingdom that will never pass away. We have to recognize which one we are contributing to.

> *"Don't store up treasures here on earth where they can erode away or may be stolen. Store them in heaven where they will never lose their value and are safe from thieves. If your profits are in heaven, your heart will be there too" (Matthew 6:19-21,* TLB*).*

If your work and your heart are invested in a heavenly vision, then what you have spent your life on will continue to matter for longer than you live. Spend your time investing in the eternal souls of people, in the eternal vision of advancing God's kingdom, and in the never-ending truth of the Gospel. In these things you will find purpose and treasure that will never be lost.

RISK

Most great things in life take some risk. We probably can each say that we've taken some pretty dumb chances in life, but we have also taken some incredible ones. Some of our risks end in disaster, but others in sheer beauty.

One thing all risk has in common is that it teaches something. We never walk away unchanged. And while stepping out and taking the risk itself is scary, we discover our own bravery in it.

Trusting God requires our faith, which is a risk. But taking a risk is necessary to follow God wholeheartedly. Of course, it's easier to sit on the sidelines. To slide under the radar. To live safe. But letting fear hold us back from taking a risk keeps us from the breathtaking possibilities of life.

The Lord is my strength and shield;
my heart trusts in him, and he helps me (Psalm 28:7, NIV).

Sometimes you just have to jump. You have to forget about the fact that it might hurt. You have to set aside what your own understanding is telling you, and trust in what God is saying. The kind of risk required for faith in God is the kind with the greatest reward.

JULY 4

GIVE ME LIBERTY

Freedom is a place without obligations. Freedom is to live exempt from debts, constraints, and bonds.

Our obligation for the sins we've committed is to satisfy justice. Our souls cannot be free without a release from our debt of sin, and the currency demanded for a soul is death. When our debt was paid by the death of Jesus, the truest form of freedom was declared over our soul. Our chains were broken, and our liberty was granted. When Jesus returned to heaven, he left his spirit with us because where his spirit is, there is freedom. (See 2 Corinthians 3:17.)

> *Now you are free from the power of sin and have become slaves of God. Now you do those things that lead to holiness and result in eternal life (Romans 6:22, NLT).*

There is a freedom waiting for you that will challenge any preconceived notions you've had of freedom. There is liberty in the presence of the Spirit of God that is unprecedented. God wants you to walk forward out of sin and into the life of freedom that he intended for you. Leave your obligation at his feet—it's taken care of.

MIRACLES

The Bible is full of exciting accounts of power, healing, and resurrection. We find ourselves wishing that we had been there when the fire of God fell upon Elijah's sacrifice, or when Lazarus stepped out of the tomb—a dead man alive again.

God is clear that miracles didn't stop when the Bible ended. His power isn't limited by the ages, and he is just as omnipotent today as he was back then—so what *is* different? Why do we feel like there are fewer miracles today? God tells us that the works he will do through his believers will be greater than the works he did through his disciples. But these works will be done in *those who believe*. God's power cannot be limited, but his display of power can be decreased by our lack of belief.

> *"Truly, truly, I say to you, whoever believes in me will also do the works that I do; and greater works than these will he do, because I am going to the Father"* (John 14:12, ESV).

God does not lie. He tells us that by believing in him, we can and will perform miracles. Believe God for something today. Don't buy into the lie that his power has been shelved; don't doubt his ability to work a miracle in your life. Believe him for something big, and ask him for it in faith, knowing that he can do it.

JULY 6

HEALING WORDS

Words can cut deeply. Isn't it amazing how many of us struggle to remember a phone number, but we can perfectly recall a string of harsh words spoken to us years ago?

Throughout the Bible, God characterizes a person of wisdom as one of few words. Perhaps this is because a careless word can do so much damage. None of us can deny that words carry power. They can easily leave a mark that is not quickly erased.

Do our words bring healing to those around us? We can't underestimate the power of our words. The beautiful thing about this next verse is that it reminds us that wise words bring *healing*.

Careless words stab like a sword,
but wise words bring healing (Proverbs 12:18, NCV*).*

If you have spoken careless words, you have the power to bring healing with new words of wisdom. If you have been pained by someone else's words, turn to the wisest words ever written—the Scriptures—to bring healing to the scars in your own heart.

THE WEIGHT OF GRACE

When the news flashes the story of a man who killed another man in cold blood, our hearts rise up within us. We become angry, almost plagued, by the injustice of what we are hearing. We wait to hear the punishment.

What if the judge laid down his gavel and announced that the murderer would not be condemned? Rather, he would be protected by the court. He would be given some consequences and then be set free under the protection of the government. That wouldn't seem quite fair, would it?

> *Then Cain said to the Lord, "This punishment is more than I can stand! Today you have forced me to stop working the ground, and now I must hide from you. I must wander around on the earth, and anyone who meets me can kill me."*
>
> *The Lord said to Cain, "No! If anyone kills you, I will punish that person seven times more." Then the Lord put a mark on Cain warning anyone who met him not to kill him (Genesis 4:13-15, NCV).*

Cain offered an unacceptable sacrifice to God, murdered his innocent brother on account of jealousy, and lied about his brother's death. Though God was grieved by Cain's sin, he showed him remarkable grace—grace in the form of an indelible mark of protection. This is the weight of grace: a grace so vast, so encompassing that even the most dreadful murderer is covered by the love and mercy of God. And it's *yours* today.

JULY 8

VOICE IN THE WILDERNESS

John the Baptist was a radical man with a fire in his belly to prepare the earth for the coming of Jesus. He didn't live for himself, but was completely sold out on the message of the Messiah. He had a thirst for eternity and an agenda to bring glory to God.

Just as John was the voice in the wilderness preparing the way for Jesus to come the first time, we now are the voice crying out to ready the world for the second coming.

> *"You yourselves know how plainly I told you, 'I am not the Messiah. I am only here to prepare the way for him.' It is the bridegroom who marries the bride, and the best man is simply glad to stand with him and hear his vows. Therefore, I am filled with joy at his success"* (John 3:28-29, NLT).

In order for Jesus to have his rightful place in the hearts of the people, John knew he had to fade away. You cannot save the people you're preaching to. You can't rescue them from sin or keep them from hell. Only Jesus can do that. But you *can* prepare the way in their hearts for his presence. Don't keep the glory of God shut up! Let it out and make him known, so that when he comes, those who have known you will know who he is because you proclaimed him clearly.

HIDDEN BEAUTY

Beauty is a powerful influencer in the lives of women. We are constantly bombarded with images and messages of what beauty is and what it should be. Even if we are confident in who we are, it can still be difficult not to give in to the subtle thoughts of not being good enough.

The awful truth about outward beauty is that no matter how much time, attention, and investment you put into it, beauty can never really last. Our appearance inevitably changes over time, and our physical beauty does fade.

In a world where we are constantly told to beautify ourselves so we will be noticed, the concept of adorning the hidden person of the heart sounds almost make-believe. But what it comes down to is the truth that the most important opinion we should seek is the opinion of our Creator. It might sound trite or cliché, but when we step away from the distraction of the media circus and all the lies it's told us, the truth becomes clear.

Let your adorning be the hidden person of the heart with the imperishable beauty of a gentle and quiet spirit, which in God's sight is very precious (1 Peter 3:4, ESV*).*

You were made to delight the heart of God. Nothing delights him more than your heart, turned toward your Savior and clothed in the imperishable beauty of a peaceful spirit flowing with gentleness, kindness, and goodness.

JULY 10

PLAYING MAKE-BELIEVE

We all played our fair share of make-believe as little girls, twirling around the room in a fancy dress-up gown or running through the fields with a wild tale alive in our minds. Every little girl probably had those long summer evenings of chasing fireflies and catching dreams, or playing hide-and-go seek and finding destiny. Our starry-eyed youth took our imaginations on the wildest of journeys as our hearts pounded with the creations of our souls.

Pretending we are someone else, or *somewhere* else, begins early in childhood and more subtly continues as we age. We still allow imagination to transport us to other places, and other circumstances. Somehow it is easier for us to embrace the wonder of "what if" than the realty of "what is."

> *I know that there is nothing better for people than to be happy and to do good while they live. That each of them may eat and drink, and find satisfaction in all their toil—this is the gift of God (Ecclesiastes 3:12-13, NIV).*

It cannot be put more clearly. There is nothing better than to be happy in your life. Your life is made up of *now*. Each moment you live, each breath you take, it's right this very second. To find happiness in your life is to find the best thing. And to find satisfaction in your effort is to find the gift of God. Treasure your life! Be satisfied with where you are. Satisfaction is living each day as if it were the dream.

THE SPICE RACK

Anyone who does any amount of cooking has a spice rack—that one place where all seasonings are kept within easy reach of the stovetop. There are some spices that get used consistently: garlic, salt, and pepper. And there are other spices that may only be used once in a while: cardamom, tarragon, anise. While those lesser-used spices may collect dust in the back of our spice cupboards, we still rely on them to bring out just the right flavor in that one particular meal.

Life is a lot like a spice rack. We shelve our experiences like spices: some make so much sense—like salt and pepper—we pull from them often, clearly recognizing their usefulness. Other experiences are more subtle and undeclared; sometimes we go years never understanding why we had them. But then, in one moment, our life recipe will call for a little saffron. And all at once, it will make so much sense. That experience we had—the one we thought we must've had by mistake—will be the only one that matters for that moment.

We know that in everything God works for the good of those who love him. They are the people he called, because that was his plan (Romans 8:28, NCV).

Maybe you have a season in your life that you often wonder about. You might look at that time and only see failure or waste. When you can't make sense of why it happened, remember that God will work it *all* for his good because you love him.

JULY 12

SURRENDER

Surrender is offering what you have to someone else without reservation. Once you surrender something, you give up your ownership and your rights along with it. What does a life fully-surrendered to Christ look like? It's holding nothing back from God, and surrendering every single part to him.

Full surrender to a holy God cannot be fabricated. God, the omniscient one, cannot be fooled by eloquent words or false commitment. Complete surrender to him can be nothing less than sincere, legitimate, full abandonment.

> *"Those of you who do not give up everything you have cannot be my disciples"* (Luke 14:33, NIV).

Being a disciple of Christ requires complete and total surrender of everything you have and everything you are. He is not asking you to give up anything that he wasn't willing to give for you. When he gave up the glory and rights of his heavenly throne, he surrendered more for you than you ever could for him. Jesus never sold this life as being casual, simple, or inexpensive. But he did promise that the reward would be great.

IDOLATRY

It's easy to think of idolatry as a distant issue, defined by people in foreign clothing bowing before intricately carved literal idols. But idolatry isn't limited to a physical, obvious idol. Idolatry is extreme devotion to something or someone.

We can be consumed with admiration for many things. Idolatry can take a million forms in our lives. Idols are simply things that take the number one place in our hearts that should belong to God alone.

Do not turn aside; for then you would go after empty things which cannot profit or deliver, for they are nothing (1 Samuel 12:21, NKJV).

Idols—whether money, a person, a career, or a dream—cannot deliver us. Only the God of the universe, who saved us with his great love, is worthy of our extreme admiration. Only he deserves our love and our reverence. Other things that we may be tempted to chase after won't give us a return or profit. Examine your heart and ask yourself the hard questions. Is God sitting exclusively on the throne of your heart? Or are there other things there that have taken his place as the object of your most extreme passion and affection?

TEMPTATION

When you approach God to ask for help in resisting temptation, or for forgiveness for a sin you've given into, do you feel ashamed? Do you feel like God couldn't possibly understand how you fell into that sin once again?

We know that Jesus was tempted to sin while he was here on earth, but we also know that he never gave into sin. Because he experienced temptation, he has great compassion toward us when we struggle with the desire to sin.

Great is our Lord and abundant in strength;
His understanding is infinite (Psalm 147:5, NASB).

Jesus understands your temptation to sin because he was tempted in the same ways! You have an advocate with Jesus—one who understands just how difficult it is to resist temptation because he has faced it. You can have confidence when you approach God to ask for forgiveness. He gives mercy and grace freely to those who earnestly seek it.

THE PLAN

We all like to have a map laid out for us to see every bend and every turn in the road. As Christians, we spend so much of our time searching for the "will of God."

Oftentimes when it comes to the will of God, we can, quite honestly, just miss the point. We look for what God wants us to do, but we miss out on seeing who he is. God knows what he is doing. Most of the time he won't tell you what he will do, he will just show you who he is.

> *By faith Abraham, when called to go to a place he would later receive as his inheritance, obeyed and went, even though he did not know where he was going (Hebrews 11:8,* NIV*).*

We aren't always going to know where we're headed. But the heart of God is for us to know *him*. Not to know every detail of the plan. Not to know what someone else's story is. Just to know him for who he is. The closer you are to God, the more delighted in you he will be. And isn't that our longing? For God to delight in us? When you abide in Jesus, only then can he truly accomplish his perfect will in you. Come before him today and strip away your questions and your need to know the plan. Just come before him needing to know only him. He will not withhold himself from you.

JULY 16

COVERING OFFENSE

When a close friend does something that offends us, our hurt can cause us to look for validation from someone completely outside the issue. We feel the need to process our pain, so we find a listening ear who will confirm our feelings.

By mulling the matter over both in our minds and with our words, we allow our anger to build. And the more we repeat the offense to listeners who validate us based on our side of the story, the further we travel from reconciliation. In order for love to prosper in our relationships, we must choose forgiveness over offense. We have to lay down whatever rights we felt we had in the situation and put love first—because love is of God.

> *Whoever covers an offense seeks love,*
> *but he who repeats a matter separates close friends*
> *(Proverbs 17:9, ESV).*

Next time someone offends you, instead of finding someone to commiserate with you, run to God and ask him for the strength to forgive. Choose to forgive the fault and protect your friendship rather than extending the pain by sharing it with others.

DEEP FRIENDSHIP

When your close friend confronts you about something you need to change, it can feel frustrating. Even if you know she's right, it's never easy to be told what your weaknesses are.

After one of these frustrating moments in a deep relationship, it can be natural for you to feel more drawn to other people with whom you have a surface-level friendship. You enjoy the easy-going nature of these friendships because they require far less work than the deeper ones.

Surface-level friendships may seem easier to maintain than facing the honesty that comes with a deep friendship. But they are only more appealing because we haven't gone deep enough to get to the brokenness. If we dive deeper, we will find people who are just as imperfect as everyone else.

The slap of a friend can be trusted to help you,
but the kisses of an enemy are nothing but lies
(Proverbs 27:6, NCV*).*

Value the deep relationships in your life. It's not easy to find someone who sees all of your mess and sticks around anyway. Those who are willing to tell you the hard things in order to encourage you in your walk with God are far more valuable than the friends who simply tell you what you want to hear.

JULY 18

ETERNAL PERSPECTIVE

Much emphasis is placed on figuring life out. We so easily become caught up in the here-and-now that we lose sight of the fact that life on earth is really only a blink compared to what our life will be in eternity.

Our entire agendas will shift when we begin to live with eternal perspective. Once we understand that the only things that will last are those of spiritual worth, we suddenly realize that our priorities must be adjusted. Our eternal worth must supersede our earthly value. We can be among the world's most wealthy here on earth but be headed for eternal destruction. Or we could be living paycheck to paycheck in this life and be governor of half a kingdom in the next.

> *He has made everything beautiful in its time. Also He has put eternity in their hearts, except that no one can find out the work that God does from beginning to end (Ecclesiastes 3:11, NKJV).*

You have the unique opportunity to determine how you will spend your forever life. Serve God well with your one short life on earth, so that you can live endlessly with him in glory.

THE GREATEST LOVE STORY

Think of the most beautiful love story you've ever heard. Romeo & Juliet, perhaps? Or a story of someone whose love seemed to transcend all commonality? What is the most beautiful thing about their love? Is it the poetry, whispered in soft stanzas? Or is it the beauty, the gorgeous sight they make together? Or is it the sacrifice, the things they gave up on account of love.

Love isn't easy because it requires sacrifice. True love requires laying something down for the sake of the one you love. Jesus laid down everything for us: his life, his glory, his deity, and his rights. He was the only person who was capable to condemn an entire human race, and he chose to condemn himself. We don't have a star-crossed lover who died in vain for a love story that would end in tragedy. Our lover is victorious and strong.

Christ had no sin, but God made him become sin so that in Christ we could become right with God (2 Corinthians 5:21, NCV).

Jesus knew that unless he laid down his life, he couldn't be with us. His love for us is so deep that he cannot face eternity without us. You will never hear a greater love story. Jesus longs for you with a fervor that led him to his death. Respond to him today by allowing your heart to be romanced in his presence.

JULY 20

STUBBORN HEARTS

Stubbornness is a tricky attribute. There is often no opening for conversation with a stubborn person. They have their own idea about how things should be done, and they aren't usually willing to listen to the advice of others.

We can all tend to be stubborn in certain ways. Unfortunately, our stubbornness sometimes comes out toward God. We feel his Spirit gently advising us, but we rationalize it away in our heads instead of allowing it to guide our hearts. God can do more in a month with a life fully surrendered to him than he can do in years with a life that's holding back.

> *"I am the Lord your God,*
> *who brought you up out of the land of Egypt.*
> *Open your mouth wide, and I will fill it.*
> *But my people did not listen to my voice;*
> *Israel would not submit to me.*
> *So I gave them over to their stubborn hearts,*
> *to follow their own counsels"* (Psalm 81:10-12, ESV).

Is there any area in your life in which you have a stubborn heart toward God? Don't forget what he has done for you. God wants to fill your mouth and use your life, but you have to open it up to him. Don't hold back. Give him every part of you, and follow his counsel rather than your own.

CHOSEN AND CALLED

When God asks us to do something, our first instinct is often to look around at who we feel could do it better. We wonder why God didn't choose that person, who—in our eyes—is clearly more qualified than we are.

God could have chosen anyone to be his mouthpiece and his leader for the incredible work he did with the Israelites. He picked Moses. He knew what Moses' strengths and weaknesses were before he called him. And he still picked Moses.

> *Moses said to the Lord, "Please, Lord, I have never been a skilled speaker. Even now, after talking to you, I cannot speak well. I speak slowly and can't find the best words" (Exodus 4:10, NCV).*

Do you ever feel like God shouldn't have picked you for something? Do you think it would have been smarter for him to pick someone who is more creative, more intelligent, or more eloquent? You may not understand why God picked you for a certain task, but you can trust that when he calls you to do something, it's because he knows that you are not only capable, you are the one he wants to do the job.

JULY 22

THINGS YOU DO NOT KNOW

"If you're there God, give me a sign!" People have screamed this into the heavens many times throughout the years. We want to see something that will tell us that God is real—and not just real, but also present. We want that experience that will bring heaven to earth and expel our doubt with a single lightning bolt.

God is more than able to give us those miraculous signs as we have seen countless times throughout the Bible and throughout history. But he is so much *more* than experience. We mistakenly think experience is the peak of his power. Other gods can perform miracles and deliver experiences, but the one true God continues to show his power in the valley. He is even in the valley of the shadow of death where miracles seem non-existent. Those other gods have nothing to offer us in despair.

> *"Thus says the LORD who made it, the LORD who formed it to establish it (the LORD is His name): 'Call to Me, and I will answer you, and show you great and mighty things, which you do not know'" (Jeremiah 33:2-3, NKJV).*

God will show us things we don't even know! We limit him to our experience and what we presently know of both him and of life. He will show us great and mighty things. God is not limited by time, space, or human understanding. Put your hope and faith in the God who *is*.

JULY 23

SUSTAINED

There is always something to worry about, isn't there? Whether it's health, finances, relationships, or details, there are many unknowns in life that can easily keep us worrying. But what if we stopped worrying? What if we stopped questioning and decided instead to feel peace? What if we could trust completely that God would take care of us and our loved ones. God is our rock and he alone will sustain us.

The words in Psalm 3 can bring us comfort and peace when we are fearful. It speaks volumes about the grace of God: the protection and safety of his hand. But the verse goes beyond peace and comfort to the *power* of God. We only wake up because of his sustaining power. When we trust and believe in this God who possesses the power of life and death, what do we have to fear? Our entire lives are in his hands. We can't change that fact, so we might as well rest in it.

I lay down and slept;
I awoke, for the Lord sustains me (Psalm 3:5, NASB).

There will be many unknowns in your life. There will be moments when the rug feels as though it's been pulled out from under you, and there is nothing to do but despair. In those moments that you can't control, you *can* trust. You can rest your soul, your mind, and your body in the hands of the one who has the power to sustain you.

JULY 24

GENEROSITY

There is need everywhere we look. Families who need homes, missionaries who need support, food shelves that need donations, and non-profit organizations that need finances. But how can we even begin to meet those needs? How could we possibly give enough to make a difference?

Generosity can be scary. Giving might mean that *we* will have to do without. Giving costs us something. We think that we have to have less in order to do more. But in God's economy, he who gives generously will be repaid lavishly. He who holds nothing back will inherit everything.

Give freely and become more wealthy;
be stingy and lose everything.
The generous will prosper;
those who refresh others will themselves be refreshed
(Proverbs 11:24-25, NLT).

God will provide for your every need, no matter how much you give to others. He doesn't measure wealth the way we do. He doesn't operate on our economic system. He gives with rewards that will last forever, and wealth that will never run out.

CHRISTIAN UNITY

As Christians, we tend to draw dividing lines in the church. We separate over doctrinal differences, worship preferences, and personal choices. We too often major on the minors, and lose sight of Jesus' powerful vision for his church. By drawing these dividing lines, we are turning on our teammates and inhibiting our corporate calling.

> *"I pray for these followers, but I am also praying for all those who will believe in me because of their teaching. Father, I pray that they can be one. As you are in me and I am in you, I pray that they can also be one in us. Then the world will believe that you sent me. I have given these people the glory that you gave me so that they can be one, just as you and I are one. I will be in them and you will be in me so that they will be completely one. Then the world will know that you sent me and that you loved them just as much as you loved me" (John 17:20-23, NCV).*

Strive to walk in unity with your brothers and sisters in Christ. Walk in love with them so that the world will see your love as the evidence of Christ in you. Take time today to read the rest of John 17, and allow Jesus' heart and prayer for the church to become yours.

JULY 26

STUMBLING IN THE DARK

Have you ever walked somewhere in the pitch black? You bump into things, knock stuff over, and often can't even place where you are or where you're going. Everything becomes muddled in the darkness. Without light to guide us, we can't see where we're going, or what we're running into.

Many times throughout the Bible, God likens being in sin to being in darkness. When we immerse ourselves in sin, thus rejecting the light of the truth, we can no longer see what we are running into. The darkness will cloud our thinking and our rationale, and we won't even be able to determine what sins are coming our way. By allowing sinful messages to enter our souls through different avenues, we lose our ability to navigate our lives.

The Word gave life to everything that was created,
and his life brought light to everyone.
The light shines in the darkness,
and the darkness can never extinguish it (John 1:4-5, NLT*).*

When wickedness begins to overtake your life, you lose the ability to recognize what is making you sin. Strive to keep your soul sensitive to the truth. Keep sight of the light by spending time in God's Word.

VICTORY

Have you ever watched one of those movie battle scenes where the good guys are grossly outnumbered? You wince as the evil army swoops in with thousands of troops carrying sophisticated weapons. While the good army has a lot of heart, you know they don't stand much of a chance. But when it all seems lost, there is that moment when, out of nowhere, reinforcements arrive in a surge of hope to assist the good army. Suddenly, they go from losing terribly to winning victoriously!

Daily, we are engaged in our own battle against sin. Left to ourselves, we don't have the strength necessary to win the fight. But when it seems all hope is lost, *our* reinforcement—Jesus Christ—arrives, and we gain the strength to boldly obtain the victory over sin.

> *Thank God! He gives us victory over sin and death through our Lord Jesus Christ.*
> *So, my dear brothers and sisters, be strong and immovable (1 Corinthians 15:57-58,* NLT*).*

You may go through seasons in your life when you feel like sin has you outnumbered. Temptation is great, and you don't feel that you have the strength to overcome it. But know that you don't have to fight alone. You have the power of God on your side, and he has already won against sin and death!

JULY 28

MEAN GIRLS

Mean girls. We have all met them, been them, or been hurt by them. Women don't have to wonder much about the definition of this term because we coined it. Somewhere along the way, we got the idea that putting another woman down would elevate us. Whether we criticize her appearance, her personality, or her situation, we are somehow under the impression that we will improve as she deteriorates.

By engaging in the mean-girl phenomenon, we are actually hindering ourselves from walking in the fullness of our salvation. What if we pulled the curtain on the whole mean-girl sham? What if we allowed ourselves to be vulnerable with one another and embraced each other with understanding? What if we chose to use kind words rather than harsh ones?

> *Get rid of your feelings of hatred. Don't just pretend to be good! Be done with dishonesty and jealousy and talking about others behind their backs. Now that you realize how kind the Lord has been to you, put away all evil, deception, envy, and fraud. Long to grow up into the fullness of your salvation; cry for this as a baby cries for his milk. (1 Peter 2:1-3,* TLB*).*

Each moment you are tempted to put down another woman, try raising her up instead. Lay down your jealousy for esteem, your criticism for compliments, and your meanness for kindness. Imagine what that would do for the body of Christ!

OUR ADVOCATE

It says in Isaiah that no matter which way we go, we will hear a voice saying, "This is the way, walk in it." But it is often so hard to hear that voice—and harder still to distinguish it from the other voices in our lives.

We stumble and fall every single day. We hear wrong, and we miss the mark continuously. We fall into sin when all we were chasing after was righteousness, and we feel guilt even when we know we've been given grace. We must rest in the fact that our God is gracious, that he knows our humanity, and that he compensates for it.

> *My little children, I am writing these things to you so that you may not sin. But if anyone does sin, we have an advocate with the Father, Jesus Christ the righteous (1 John 2:1,* ESV*).*

You have a mediator between yourself and the almighty God. It is someone who loved you enough to lay down everything for you. Surely a man who loves you with that kind of intensity also loves you enough to forgive your imperfections?

JULY 30

LOVE AT FIRST

"How did the two of you meet?" We ask the inevitable question, starry-eyed, knowing the romance and dreamy memories that will tumble out. Every love story has a beginning—a first look, a first word, a first thought—the creation of love itself.

What does the beginning of your love story with God look like? Was there a song that you can remember falling in love with him to? Maybe there was a verse—a word from his very mouth that captured your heart. Or is there something about the place you were in when your heart responded to his and you walked away changed? It's all too easy to lose the initial passion of love. God becomes woven into our lives like a single thread in a tapestry, and like that, though he is part of us, he isn't the whole substance.

"I have this against you, that you have abandoned the love you had at first" (Revelation 2:4, ESV).

Search your heart today. Have you abandoned the depth of love you had at first? Have you strayed from that place where all you wanted was him and all you needed was his presence? Take some time to quiet your heart today and remember everything about the moment in which you fell in love with God. Sometimes we have to remember how we fell in love to remind ourselves that we *are* in love.

PEOPLE OF TRUTH

Have you ever met someone who speaks hard-hitting truth every time you talk to them? They seem to be soaked in the presence of God, and you know that when you hear them speak, you will be ministered to by the power of the Holy Spirit through them. These people echo the heart of God because they study the Word of God.

If we meditate on truth, we will become people of truth. If we read the Bible constantly, truth will flow out of us—along with joy, peace and wisdom. Even in our normal conversations we will find ourselves using phrases that are directly from Scripture. That's what God wants. He wants his praise and his words to be continually on our lips—a never-ending worship service to him as we speak.

This Book of the Law shall not depart from your mouth, but you shall meditate in it day and night, that you may observe to do according to all that is written in it. For then you will make your way prosperous, and then you will have good success (Joshua 1:8, NKJV).

If you are constantly in the Word—inundating your soul, your spirit, and your mind with the power of God—then the power of God is what will resurface when you open your mouth and speak to others. His goodness, kindness, mercy, and grace will flow out of you, and you will become a person of truth.

To enjoy your work and to accept your lot in life—that is indeed a gift from God. The person who does that will not need to look back with sorrow on his past, for God gives him joy.

Ecclesiastes 5:20 TLB

PLANNER

The month of August is one that creates a sense of eager anticipation. Summer is wrapping up, and with September usually comes new beginnings. There is excitement in the air as the school buses start up their engines, sports seasons get underway, and Labor Day plans come and go. August can be a great time to get into a routine.

August can mean that your mornings start just a half hour early to spend time in the presence of God. Or you find time in the afternoon to go for a quick walk to pray. Or you start a prayer chain with women you know to pray for one another as the months roll by. When you make dedicated time with the Lord, conversing with him becomes a part of your every day—a necessity to find your day complete. And oh, how it delights him when we spend time in his presence!

> *Now devote your heart and soul to seeking the LORD your God. Begin to build the sanctuary of the LORD God, so that you may bring the ark of the covenant of the LORD and the sacred articles belonging to God into the temple that will be built for the Name of the LORD" (1 Chronicles 22:19, NIV).*

What could a different routine look like for you? How might you make it more intentional in meeting the Lord?

AUGUST 2

GRATITUDE

Have you ever noticed on vacation that your heart feels lighter? That you worry less and are more thankful? Cultivating a heart of thankfulness can shift our entire perspective on life. When we are grateful, we start to see the light of God so much more. We start to see him *everywhere*.

A thankful heart is a heart that refuses to let the enemy in and deceive us. Suddenly, our circumstances seem not so terrible, our problems not so huge. A heart of gratitude glorifies God and keeps us centered on him. Just like on vacation, you can have that same perspective every day—even in the most mundane circumstances.

> *Whatever you do, whether in word or deed, do it all in the name of the Lord Jesus, giving thanks to God the Father through him (Colossians 3:17, NIV).*

What can you do to start cultivating a heart of gratitude? A heart of thankfulness keeps you grounded in Christ, in communion with him, and allows you to live the fullest life he's designed for you.

HEART CENTER

Social media: an escape, a gift, a communicative tool, a joy stealer, a comparison thief, a comedian, entertainment. Social media can be fun! But it can also become an idol when we don't recognize it as such. Suddenly, instead of opening up our Bible, we are clicking on our phones checking Facebook, posting photos and status updates to seek attention and approval from people rather than our Creator.

God's desire for our life is that we chose him above all else. He wants to be our focal point, one we return to time and again, so we don't ever steer too far off course. Instead of seeking approval from others, let's turn our eyes toward the one who loves us most, whose voice is the only one we should hear.

> *If then you have been raised with Christ, seek the things that are above, where Christ is, seated at the right hand of God. Set your minds on things that are above, not on things that are on earth (Colossians 3:1-2,* ESV*).*

Where do you choose to spend the majority of your time? What choices could you eliminate to stay centered on Jesus? In a busy life of choices, it's important to know your back-up is also your best option—seeking God and choosing life with him.

AUGUST 4

THE VOICE OF LOVE

When we live for other voices, we will quickly become worn out and discouraged. Other people's expectations for how we should live, act, and be are sometimes unreachable. There is one voice that matters, and it can come in a variety of forms—the voice of God.

What God would tell us is that we are loved, we are cherished, and we have significant value. We are his beloved, his daughters, his beautiful creation. This is the voice that matters. This is the voice to come back to when we feel like we're not enough.

> *"The Father gives me the people who are mine. Every one of them will come to me, and I will always accept them" (John 6:37,* NCV*).*

What are the voices you typically listen to? Can you ignore them and focus only on the voice that matters? He will encourage you and remind you that you *are* enough. Nothing you do or don't do is going to make him love you any more or any less. Soak it in, so you can drown out all the other voices.

AUGUST 5

RISK-TAKER

There will be opportunities that arise that might be surprising to us. We might suddenly be presented with something that feels kind of terrifying. We view it as an opportunity because we see the benefit in it somewhere along the way. We understand that it could be as much of a gift to our lives as a potentially difficult ride or transition before the gift appears.

Stepping through the unknown takes courage, and courage isn't always readily available. Through the power of prayer, and wrestling with the opportunity's positives and negatives, hopefully we come to the point where our hearts feel the peace we've been looking for. That makes the task of accepting the opportunity much easier.

Your word is a lamp to guide my feet
and a light for my path (Psalm 119:105, NLT).

Have you taken a risk and been pleasantly surprised by the outcome? How do you fully give your trust to God? You still might not feel brave about a decision, but you can trust the peace in your heart. That alone takes courage. This opportunity might be one of the biggest surprises of your life; it's wonderful and scary, but perfect for you.

AUGUST 6

BREAK EVERY CHAIN

There is a chance to start over—every day if we need to. From the inside out, we can be transformed and our hearts renewed. We can essentially remake ourselves with the help, healing, and transformative nature of Christ! Jesus died on the cross to promise us a life free from the bondage of sin, free from hopelessness, free from any chains that try to trap us. In Christ, we are set free.

We need to hear the truth of Christ's promise for us and stop the cycle of hopelessness, defeat, and bondage to sin. All we need to do is get on our knees and pray.

> *"His purpose in all of this is that they should seek after God, and perhaps feel their way toward him and find him—though he is not far from any one of us"* (Acts 17:27, TLB).

Is there an area of your life that you need to receive freedom from? Wait for God's voice to permeate the deepest, saddest parts of you. He wants you to let him take care of you. He is pursuing your heart.

FAITH OR SIGHT?

Sometimes we demand a lot of God. "God, I'd like this house," "God, this is my dream job," "I'm so ready to have a husband," and we wait in expectation. We wait for him to do the impossible. We wait for him to give us the desires of our hearts. Because if he does, then he is most definitely all-powerful. If he does, he heard your cry and answered. If he does, he loves you.

This is living by *sight.*

In 2 Corinthians it says we live by faith, not sight. We often doubt God. Living by faith is giving up any control we thought we had, and sitting in the passenger seat in eager anticipation of where God is taking us.

> *We are always confident and know that as long as we are at home in the body we are away from the Lord. For we live by faith, not by sight (2 Corinthians 5:6-7,* NIV*).*

Have you been living by faith or by sight? How can you let go of unfulfilled desires, and start living by faith? God's desires for you are great! He wants only the best for you and asks for your faith in return.

AUGUST 8

IN THE SECRET

Cherish the secret things. So much of our life is for others. *So much*. Whether it is the requirement of jobs, keeping up relationships, or the programs we volunteer for, so much of our time and energy is spent on other people.

God wants our time. He wants it for us and for him. Maybe this will require a designated prayer closet, or a quiet place away. Maybe we head outside with our Bible and journal to sneak away for a while. However we do it, our heavenly Father sees us. *He sees us!* What a faithful gift that thought alone is; he sees us in secret and will meet us where we are.

> *"When you pray, do not be like the hypocrites, for they love to pray standing in the synagogues and on the street corners to be seen by others. Truly I tell you, they have received their reward in full. But when you pray, go into your room, close the door and pray to your Father, who is unseen. Then your Father, who sees what is done in secret, will reward you" (Matthew 6:5-6,* NIV*).*

Can you get away today in secret to pray? In secret, God will reward your heart. Make sneaking away with him a daily routine.

GLORIOUS

Leaves changing from green to orange to red. Gently falling snow. A rainbow-colored sunrise. A sprout of newness in the dirt. The smell of freshly cut grass. The rustling of leaves in the trees. The smell of a pine tree at Christmas time. Billowy, moving clouds. Sunshine kissing your cheeks. It is amazing that our Creator would make all of this for us to enjoy. It's glorious, really.

Yet, days can go by and we haven't stopped to notice. We forget to slow down. We ignore this incredibly beautiful world that he made for us to explore and enjoy. It is amazing what a walk with a friend, a run through the woods, or the feel of bare feet on grass can do for our soul.

On the glorious splendor of your majesty,
and on your wondrous works, I will meditate
(Psalm 145:5, NRSV).

Do you take time to get outside and enjoy all that he created? The next time you're feeling a bit squirmy, slow down, take a walk outside, and soak in his presence that's all around you: in the grass between your toes, in the rustle of leaves above you, and in the sunshine kissing your cheeks.

AUGUST 10

WORTH HOLDING ON TO

When you find that woman who has been on most of life's journey with you—a sister, a mom, a best friend—hold on to her. When you find that woman who life is easy with—no judgment, shame, or fear of being yourself—hold on to her. When you find that woman you can laugh with, and cry with all in the same conversation—hold on to her.

Good girlfriends are wonderful to have. They get you when no one else will. They are the people you can go to for advice no matter what time it is. The Bible says that friends encourage and love each other. Those qualities are such a gift, especially when found in that friend that you can do everyday life with.

> *"This is my commandment, that you love one another as I have loved you. Greater love has no one than this, that someone lay down his life for his friends. You are my friends if you do what I command you"*
> *(John 15:12-14, ESV).*

Do you have a friend that blesses your life frequently? Are you that person for someone else? If you have a mutually beneficial friendship, hold onto it. If you don't, start being the kind of friend you need, and see what happens.

THE GAP

There are days where you might wake up a little more sluggish, with a little less energy and positivity about the day. That can feel kind of empty, a gap you're hoping to fill. The great thing about the God you serve is that in him, you can be complete. He can be that gap-filler. As you sit with him, his light begins to burn brighter.

On that particular day meet him in dependence. Come to him even when you don't feel like it. Present your helplessness and emptiness to him and he will bless you and fill your gap with warmth, joy, peace, care, and love.

"Blessed are the poor in spirit,
for theirs is the kingdom of heaven.
Blessed are those who mourn,
for they will be comforted.
Blessed are the meek,
for they will inherit the earth
Blessed are those who hunger and thirst for righteousness,
for they will be filled" (Matthew 5:3-6, NIV*).*

Have you seen the fruit of this promise on one of your rough days? When you spend time with him and allow him to speak to you, you can rest knowing you were transformed and filled on one of the hardest days. He is faithful and loving no matter our circumstance or feeling.

AUGUST 12

TRUST IN THE LITTLE THINGS

God has given us a huge gift in his faithful nature. He promises us things and sticks to those promises without fail.

It feels easier to trust God in the big moments, the desperate moments. But what about the everyday moments? The times that we grab hold of control and want to do it all ourselves. In those moments, we can press into him without restraint. Let go, cry out to him, ask him to carry you. And he will. The everyday moments that might feel crooked will be straightened. He will carry you as he promises.

> *Those who know Your name will put their trust in You;*
> *For You, Lord, have not forsaken those who seek You (Psalm 9:10, NKJV).*

How beautiful is this God! He will give you a path to confidently walk on if all you do is trust him. Where do you have the most difficulty trusting God? Practice letting go in those moments. Trust him.

SEARCH MY HEART, OH GOD

It's easy to point out someone else's sin and overlook our own. It might not be as obvious, but it's there because we are all sinners. Search your heart and find the area that needs to be pruned. The area that can sometimes feel dark. There is hope in the darkness; there is light. No matter what you've done, or what feelings you might sometimes have, there are none that cannot be overcome.

Lift your unpruned heart to the Father who created you, and ask him to bring the darkness into the light. Ask him to reveal to you where you are weak. He can make you strong. You can do this—you are a child of the one true king! You have the greatest warrior beside you, casting his light on every part of you.

> *"For a brief moment, the Lord our God has been gracious in leaving us a remnant and giving us a firm place in his sanctuary, and so our God gives light to our eyes and a little relief in our bondage" (Ezra 9:8, NIV).*

What are the areas of your life that need to be confessed? Take some time to reflect on them in prayer with God. Ask him to reveal himself to you.

AUGUST 14

LIMITLESS

Do you struggle with where you fit? Are you on a hunt to find your purpose? Do you feel like you've changed, and the purpose you thought God had for you seems vastly different now? It can be so confusing, can't it? When we think our purpose is unclear, we can easily become blind to God's capacity.

Friends, God has no capacity. We serve a God without limits. He tells us that, in him, anything is possible. You don't need to have confidence in what you can do—only in what he can accomplish through you. He is capable of absolutely anything, and his plans for you run deep.

Again and again they limited God, preventing him from blessing them.
Continually they turned back from him
and wounded the Holy One!
They forgot his great love, how he took them by his hand
and with redemption's kiss he delivered them from their enemies (Psalm 78:41-42, TPT*).*

What do you feel your purpose is? Open your heart and mind to a limitless God. Believe, deep in your heart, the fullness of his limitless capability for you. Pray on that, take steps, and watch him fulfill your meaningful purpose.

UNIFIED IN ONE BODY

Generally speaking, women are relational beings. We desire closeness, raw conversation—vulnerable, real, and mature relationships. In the same breath, sometimes we are the ones who make those relationships so hard to form. We judge, we compare, we stay on the surface to protect ourselves.

There is a reason we are created the way we are. God is not naïve about women. His desire is a unified body. Black, red, yellow, green, single, married, rich, poor… there is no boundary for us to be in relation with one another. Instead of making assumptions about others and jumping to conclusions, love, be trustworthy, reach out, go deep, and be gracious in your heart toward others. We can be a blessing to each other.

> *I appeal to you, dear brothers and sisters, by the authority of our Lord Jesus Christ, to live in harmony with each other. Let there be no divisions in the church. Rather, be of one mind, united in thought and purpose (1 Corinthians 1:10, NLT).*

Are there women in your life that you want to go deep with but have held back from? Are there women you might have judged that need a second chance? Take a risk. Reach out. Grab coffee together.

AUGUST 16

RELEASING BEAUTY

God provides us relief from any bondage we carry. He truly does. Our Father can take any mistake we've made in the past and release the beauty in that error. We don't need to be so hard on ourselves. We don't need to feel trapped, or think we've failed, or hold on so tightly that we can't see the joy in our current circumstance.

Turn your face toward God and let him break that bondage apart. He can take the journey and form it into a place of humility and empathy for others. Watch as the chains break and you walk away much, much lighter.

> *Therefore, since we are surrounded by such a great cloud of witnesses, let us throw off everything that hinders and the sin that so easily entangles. And let us run with perseverance the race marked out for us, fixing our eyes on Jesus, the pioneer and perfecter of faith. For the joy set before him he endured the cross, scorning its shame, and sat down at the right hand of the throne of God* (Hebrews 12:1-2, NIV).

What are the mistakes you've made in the past that you have trouble letting go of? Take a few minutes to let his promise of redemption make way into your heart. And then forgive yourself.

AUGUST 17

ROOTS

Have you ever tried to nurture a plant in a pot? It can flourish with persistent watering, moving it to the right temperature and light, and pruning it when it gets too big. Usually it grows straight up since the pot restricts the roots from growing too wide. Up and up it grows. But if you forget about it for a while, not caring for it the way it was designed to be cared for, it can start to brown, wither, and eventually, it will die.

Roots. They make all the difference in health. Roots take shape underground, where you can't see. Often roots show the true health of anything we examine. We should have deep roots in our heart's devotion to God. *Deep* doesn't mean a long history; it means that what happens in our homes, our hearts, and our relationships are nourishing and pleasing to God.

> *"They will be like a tree planted by the water*
> *that sends out its roots by the stream…*
> *and never fails to bear fruit"* (Jeremiah 17:8, NIV).

Where is your heart health today, spiritually speaking? Do you need persistent watering and nourishment? Take the time today to ask God for that and watch as your roots come alive. When you feel you're getting a little brown or wilted, just go to the caretaker and start again. Each time you do, your roots grow a little stronger.

AUGUST 18

JUST SAY NO

Are you in a pattern of always saying yes? Afraid of letting others down? Sometimes saying yes can feel really good… until it doesn't.

When we long to say no—when we crave a moment of peace or a commitment-free week—that list of yes items can seem like an unattainable mountain. Constantly saying yes leads to an exhausted woman and a less-than-our-best self. Carrying that feeling around is much worse than choosing to say no.

> *Our people must learn to devote themselves to doing what is good, in order to provide for urgent needs and not live unproductive lives (Titus 3:14,* NIV*).*

In what areas of your life do you crave more space? Pray for the courage to say no when you need to. Making time for yourself is admirable; desiring more margin in your life for simplicity is okay—that is something to say yes to.

AUGUST 19

THE WAR

There is a war going on right in front of you. A deep, big, all-in battle for *you*—for your heart. The war is raging and has been since you were born. There is one that desires goodness for you. There is one that loves you unconditionally and wants to see you become who he designed. There is one that has sacrificed for you, died for you, bled for you. There is one that not only takes but also gives away, freely. There is one that calls you daughter, calls you his beloved.

Do not let the other one win. Do not give in. Instead, look up. Stop and sit in silence. Listen to the truth whispered in your heart. Let it go deep. Let it settle. *You are loved. Cherished. Beautiful. I am yours and you are mine. I hear you. I love you…without fail, without border. There is nothing you can do to separate yourself from my love. I am yours…forever.*

> *Be alert and of sober mind. Your enemy the devil prowls around like a roaring lion looking for someone to devour. Resist him, standing firm in the faith…And the God of all grace…will himself restore you and make you strong, firm and steadfast (1 Peter 5:8-10, NIV).*

Do you grasp the spiritual warfare that goes on in your life and recognize it for what it is? Continue to press into God and his Word to create your armor.

AUGUST 20

GOD'S EAR

God hears you. Whether you are shouting praises of thanksgiving, crying tears of mourning, or singing phrases of glory, God hears. He listens. He does not abandon or ignore.

He hears your voice. He hears your heart. He hears your shouts, your whispers, and your thoughts. Sometimes this seems scary; we feel like we have to perform. That is a lie. Do not believe it. God takes us as we are, where we are. We don't have to filter, pretend, or please. He meets us, loves us, accepts us just as we are in this moment.

I love the LORD, for he heard my voice;
he heard my cry for mercy.
Because he turned his ear to me,
I will call on him as long as I live…
Then I called on the name of the LORD:
"LORD, save me!"
The LORD is gracious and righteous;
our God is full of compassion.
The LORD protects the unwary;
when I was brought low, he saved me.
Return to your rest, my soul,
for the LORD has been good to you (Psalm 116: 1-7, NIV).

Do you believe God hears you? What do you want to tell him right now? He is a beautiful, caring God who takes us as sinners and holds our hand as we walk the path to salvation.

AUGUST 21

UNDENIABLE TRUST

Have you heard a personal story that has made you weep? Have you watched as that person overcame undeniable odds and still clung to Jesus? Were you in awe or did you have confidence that you would react the same in a tragedy or difficult situation? Our response to shattered dreams is incredibly important in our spiritual walk. No matter how we feel, our job is to have complete trust and confidence that God is with us, walking right alongside us, holding our hand.

We are called to love him even when it feels like he's not there. We are called to be faithful even when it doesn't feel like he's faithful back. He is. Trusting in God is pleasing to him. He does the rest of the work for us. Isn't that beautiful? We have to let go and trust him in the wake of shattered dreams. God will take our hand and lead us, doing the hard work for us.

> *"Surely I am with you always, to the very end of the age" (Matthew 28:20,* NIV*).*

Have you had a tough circumstance where you've had to press into God like never before? How did you respond? He wants you to reach out to him in those hard moments. His love is the best remedy.

AUGUST 22

REST IN JESUS

Have you ever been awake when you think no one else is? Maybe you had an early morning flight, and you feel you are the only person who could possibly be stirring at that hour. It feels kind of magical, doesn't it? It's like you have an unshared secret. Regardless of you being a night owl, morning person, or somewhere in-between, there is peace that comes with meeting Jesus in secret—when your world has stopped for a bit.

Whatever it looks like, rising early or staying up late, taking a work break, a study break, or a mommy break, finding that quiet is where you can actually acquire strength. We need spiritual food to conquer each day.

He who dwells in the secret place of the Most High
Shall abide under the shadow of the Almighty
(Psalm 91:1, NKJV).

Can you find daily quiet time to meet with Jesus? He will meet you in that space, filling you with peace, strength, and love to go out and conquer the world.

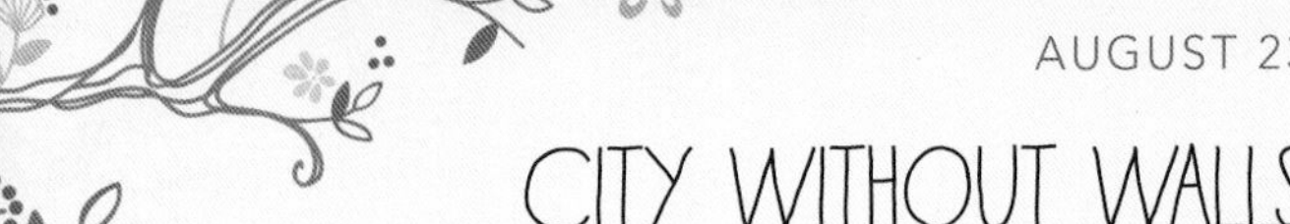

AUGUST 23

CITY WITHOUT WALLS

In grade school, we had to wait to speak until our hand was raised. The teacher would not call on a single student until she had finished talking. The children could barely wait another second before blurting out the answer. These teachers were wise. They were trying to teach self-control—a valuable life lesson.

Lack of self-control comes in a variety of forms: overeating, spending too much time on the computer or phone, losing our tempers, wasting money, gossiping, and the list goes on. Self-control requires discipline. In order to perfect it, we need to practice and ask God for help. Proverbs 25:28 describes a man without self-control as a city broken into and left without walls. What an easy way to let the enemy in.

> *The grace of God has appeared that offers salvation to all people. It teaches us to say "No" to ungodliness and worldly passions, and to live self-controlled, upright and godly lives in this present age (Titus 2:11-12,* NIV*).*

Which areas in your life require you to practice more self-control? Who can you be accountable to? Ask for help today in the area of self-control. Bring your weakness into the light and find the help you need in the Lord.

AUGUST 24

A HEART FOR OUR SISTER

Have you ever felt like you were split-second judged? You had an encounter, it didn't go as planned, and immediately you felt less than ideal. We desire grace for ourselves when we are having a "bad day," but it's so easy to forget to extend that same grace to others. Maybe we've done it for so long that we don't even realize we are doing it.

Here is what we need to remember: we are the same. We are daughters of the Most High God, precious, beautifully made in his image. We belong to Jesus. Let us ask God to give us hearts to see women for who they are—sisters—and remember they are nothing less than we are.

> *By the grace given to me I say to everyone among you not to think of himself more highly than he ought to think, but to think with sober judgment, each according to the measure of faith that God has assigned (Romans 12:3,* ESV*).*

Have you had a recent encounter where you've judged someone or haven't extended grace? Reflect on the women in your life and your heart toward them. Ask God to give you eyes to see them as he does.

CHANGE OF SEASON

You will, undoubtedly, have various seasons in your life: seasons of longing and contentment, seasons of discouragement and joy, seasons of more and less. Being a grown-up means stretching into new ways of living, and this usually doesn't happen until the season hits.

Seasons can be challenging. They require bravery, obedience, dedication, and sometimes total upheaval of everything comfortable in our lives. If we feel that impending corner of a season change in our hearts, it usually means God is preparing us for something different—a *change*. In those seasons of life, the one who won't change, won't back down, and won't leave us stranded is our heavenly Father.

> *"Be strong and courageous, and act; do not fear nor be dismayed, for the LORD God, my God, is with you. He will not fail you nor forsake you until all the work for the service of the house of the LORD is finished"* (1 Chronicles 28:20, NASB).

Do you see an impending season change approaching? How does it make you feel? Be brave! God will not move you into something without giving you the grace you need to make it through.

AUGUST 26

JUST REST

Picture a season in your life where you were knee-deep in busyness, swallowed in sadness, or buried in exhaustion. Picture that season and how you looked, acted, reacted, and survived. Now picture Jesus. See his face, feel his warmth, envision his smile. Picture yourself back in that same tiresome season, sitting on a chair in your house, desiring to spend time with God but being so extremely tired that you couldn't find the strength. So you sit.

Here comes Jesus walking toward you. You invite him to come closer but are ready with the excuses and reasons for why you have been absent from him. He walks toward you and outstretches his hand. When he reaches you, his hand starts to move toward your head. Gently, ever so lovingly, he pushes your head to the chair back, and whispers, "Rest, Daughter, just rest."

The Lord will give strength to His people;
The Lord will bless His people with peace (Psalm 29:11, NKJV).

Have you encountered a moment with Jesus where you understood more fully that he gets you to your very core? He knows your heart. He knows when your soul needs rest. Let him stroke your hair and sing you a lullaby.

PEACE LIKE A RIVER

Where do you usually go to find peace? Is there a certain place? A certain person? One of the greatest gifts of God is his undeniable, unfathomable peace. It is a deep well that comes with knowing and experiencing Jesus' love. No matter where we are, where we are going, and whatever we might be experiencing, his peace is greater.

Come, Lord Jesus, come.

Grasp how deep his well runs. Lasting peace and joy does not come in the world or people around you. Although those can be comforting, true, transforming, and powerful peace can only come from our Father. And oh, how he loves when we come to his well.

"I am the Lord your God,
who teaches you what is best for you,
who directs you in the way you should go
...your peace would have been like a river,
your well-being like the waves of the sea"
(Isaiah 48:17-18, NIV).

Where do you usually turn for peace? Have you experienced the indescribable peace of God?

AUGUST 28

HEALER

Whether you are carrying pain and suffering from past abuse or tragedy, or you've more recently been hurt, run toward the one who heals. There is no requirement or need too great; he will piece you back together.

It might take work. It will take constant communion with him to remind you of his healing power, but he will glue you back until you are whole. Broken souls, broken bodies, broken sisters, be reminded of his power in these moments and do not turn away.

Hallelujah! Praise the Lord!
How beautiful it is when we sing our praises
to the beautiful God;
for praise makes you lovely before him
and brings him great delight!
He heals the wounds of every shattered heart
(Psalm 147:1, 3, TPT).

Are you experiencing pain and need God's healing power? Release everything you are holding onto and let him heal you.

BELT OF TRUTH

In 2 Timothy, it says that we were not given a spirit of fear. Fear comes from the enemy and when we choose to give into that fear, we are giving the enemy power over us. By believing his lies, we give him his greatest weapon. Instead, expose the lie for what it is.

This isn't always easy. It can take repetition in prayer time with Jesus and constant communion with him to be reminded. But the truth will prevail and you can start to change your anxious, fearful heart into a heart that feels powerful in love and truth.

> *Stand firm then, with the belt of truth buckled around your waist, with the breastplate of righteousness in place, and with your feet fitted with the readiness that comes from the gospel of peace (Ephesians 6:14-15, NIV).*

Where do you struggle with fear? Defeat the enemy's power over that fear by turning it over to the truth and handing it to Jesus.

AUGUST 30

JOYOUS JOURNEY

There is great joy in the journey: in the mundane details, in the difficult times, in the confusing moments, and in the tears. There is so much joy to be found in the quiet and in the noise.

Pity parties and comparisons create a direct path for the enemy to steal our joy. There is hope in Jesus and the gift of little joy-filled moments. They come in varying forms: sunshine rays pouring in the windows, a nice person at the check-out counter, a turn-the-radio-as-high-as-it-can-go kind of song, a dance party in the living room, or the taste of a delicious meal after a long day. Whatever the moment, there is joy if we look for it.

> *Consider it pure joy, my brothers and sisters, whenever you face trials of many kinds, because you know that the testing of your faith produces perseverance. Let perseverance finish its work so that you may be mature and complete, not lacking anything (James 1:2-4,* NIV*).*

There's a journey of joy in waking up every day knowing it's another day to breathe in the fresh air, head to dinner with a girlfriend, or grab coffee with a co-worker. Find joy in the moment.

THE RACE

We are running this race to win a prize that is far greater than we could ever know. Our Lord was obedient until death with what he was meant to do. However, he did grow overwhelmed and three times asked his father if there was another way (see Luke 22). Jesus persevered with the help of angels.

There will be times when you feel like you are slipping and times when you'll fall, but be assured, Jesus will pick you up. Continue to move forward with a steadfast heart and a desire to persevere until you have finished your race.

> *Blessed is the one who perseveres under trial because, having stood the test, that person will receive the crown of life that the Lord has promised to those who love him (James 1:12,* NIV*).*

Have there been times on your spiritual walk where you have wanted to give up? Let Jesus pick you back up and help you get back on track.

SEPTEMBER

Commit your work to the LORD,
and your plans will be established.

PROVERBS 16:3 ESV

HE KNOWS WHEN WE DON'T

You stare at the menu, overwhelmed by choices. Pasta sounds yummy, but you're avoiding gluten. Salad sounds healthy, but you just had that for lunch. Steak sounds perfect until you look at the price. Everyone else has ordered; all eyes are on you. You know you're hungry, just not what *for.* "What do I want?" you ask, though not expecting an answer.

There are days prayer can feel like that. We know we want something—we sense an ache or longing—but can't quite identify it. Other times, we're simply in too much pain to focus. We need, we need… but we can't get the words out. "What do I want?" we cry. This time, we *can* expect an answer. The Holy Spirit, because he lives inside us, knows us so intimately he can actually step in and pray on our behalf. He knows, even when we don't.

> *The Spirit helps us with our weakness. We do not know how to pray as we should. But the Spirit himself speaks to God for us, even begs God for us with deep feelings that words cannot explain (Romans 8:26,* NCV*).*

Spend some time with the Spirit today. Thank him for knowing your heart, and sharing it with God when you can't.

NO SACRIFICE

In order to prove his undying love for you, the man of your dreams just: a) quit his job and donated all his possessions to the poor—and is now living in a tent in your front yard, or b) spent twelve hours driving to see you followed by eight hours of open, honest conversation about everything from your favorite childhood memory, to your dreams, to your deepest fears. Choose one.

Just as we would not be particularly romanced by someone proving his love by surrendering his belongings, God does not want our sacrifices. We don't need to make a grand gesture, we just need to sit down and read his Word. He wants us to want *him* more than anything. He doesn't want our stuff.

> *"I don't want your sacrifices—I want your love; I don't want your offerings—I want you to know me"* (Hosea 6:6, TLB).

When you consider the only sacrifice the Lord wants from you is some of your undivided attention, that all you need to offer him is your interest, what happens in your heart? Share this with him today.

SEPTEMBER 3

PREPARE HIM ROOM

Imagine your life if all you ever did was add to your possessions. Unless we want to be featured on a certain, very popular reality television show about people with far too much stuff, bringing new things in necessitates taking old things out. We don't build a bigger closet, we go through and select which items to donate. We don't build a bigger garage, we trade the aging sedan, SUV, or minivan for a newer, better model.

So too, when we accept Christ's sacrifice and the Holy Spirit takes up residence in our hearts, we must make room. Old habits must make way for fresh, inspired new ways of being. Things like jealousy, bitterness, and insecurity need to be bagged up and taken out so that graciousness, forgiveness, and confidence can move in. As his presence grows inside us, the old ways diminish.

> *"He must become greater and greater, and I must become less and less" (John 3:30,* NLT*).*

How much space are you allowing the Holy Spirit right now, and how much are you holding onto for yourself? Is it time to clean house? What will change if you do?

SEPTEMBER 4

HUMILITY

"You did an incredible job; you're so talented!" Quick, how do you respond? Going beyond "thank you" and actually accepting—embracing—the kind words being spoken about us is difficult for many. As little girls, we're told it's rude not to say "thank you" when complimented, but society, and our peers, also send an opposing message: we'd best not be perceived as agreeing. No girl wants to be labeled *vain.*

So how freeing is it to learn that everything good about us is actually about Jesus? Every good gift, from beauty to a lovely singing voice to the ability to sink a three-pointer on the basketball court, is from him. You're not full of yourself; you're full of *him!* Even better, every time we mess up is an opportunity to brag about his awesomeness. After all, we're only human. We can't do anything on our own.

If I must boast, I will boast of the things that show my weakness (2 Corinthians 11:30, NIV).

Is it easy for you to accept compliments? Identify your best qualities, considering them gifts from God. Talk freely to him about the ways he made you special, and how infinitely special you find him.

BEING KNOWN

Think of the most perfect gift you've ever received. Not the most extravagant, but the one that was just so perfectly *you* that you realized the giver really knew you. They heard you, that one time, when you mentioned that one thing, perhaps in passing, and because they were listening with their heart, they saw into yours. They get you.

We love to be "gotten," and long to be seen. For many of us it's how we know we are loved. How much, then, must the Father love us? He who knows everything about us—who takes the time to listen to every longing and comfort every sigh—is waiting to give us his perfect gifts. We are known. We are loved.

You know what I long for, Lord;
you hear my every sigh (Psalm 38:9, NLT*).*

Share your longing with God today. Let him show you his great love by revealing how intimately he knows you. Let him give you a good and perfect gift.

SEPTEMBER 6

HE IS OUR STRENGTH

The pile of bills, the noise the car is making, the layoff rumors at work, the child who stayed home sick—again. Pressures can overwhelm us, especially when they accumulate. Add in the stresses we put upon ourselves—*Am I good enough? Why did I say that? Other women's houses aren't this cluttered*—and you've got a potent recipe for insecurity.

When things seem impossible, and they often do, praise God that we have his promises and his power. It is not up to us to solve our problems; we need only to trust the Lord and accept his help.

> *Even though the fig trees have no blossoms,*
> *and there are no grapes on the vines;*
> *even though the olive crop fails,*
> *and the fields lie empty and barren;*
> *even though the flocks die in the fields,*
> *and the cattle barns are empty,*
> *yet I will rejoice in the LORD!*
> *I will be joyful in the God of my salvation! (Habakkuk 3:17-18 NLT).*

Where could you use a little, or a lot of, God's strength right now? Offer your worries to your Father.

SEPTEMBER 7

TRUE FRIENDS

Thinking back to when you were a girl, you can probably pull up a memory of a time you thought someone was your friend, only to realize you were mistaken. A revealed secret, broken promise, or perhaps a certain boy made it clear she wasn't your friend after all. Maybe you don't need to think back to your childhood. Sadly, women who are supposedly friends hurt, betray, and disappoint one another every day.

Think now of your true friends. The ones who have seen—and forgiven—your worst, and who have gotten that same grace from you. Whether you have one special friend, or a handful, they are treasures from God.

A friend loves at all times,
And a brother is born for adversity (Proverbs 17:17, NASB).

We are meant to do life together. We are meant to love one another always. Who are your "girls"? Those women who, no matter what, have your back. Thank the Lord for them today, then reach out and let them know what they mean to you.

PRIORITIES

"I went online to check one thing, and the next thing I knew, two hours had passed!" How recently have you heard—or said—something similar? Our modern world provides endless distractions, and if we're not careful, those distractions can interfere with what we want to accomplish and who we want to be. This is why we need priorities.

God's Word tells us this world is passing; today—this minute, in fact—is the only certainty. So those things we're thinking of doing *someday* or even next month, if they matter to us, we'd be wise to do them today. What matters to us? Our relationships, our careers, getting to know the Father as intimately as we can? Let's be sure we give those things our full attention—today.

A shepherd should pay close attention
to the faces of his flock
and hold close to his heart
the condition of those he cares for.
A man's strength, power, and riches
will one day fade away,
not even nations endure forever
(Proverbs 27:23-24, TPT).

What are your priorities? Would they be obvious to someone observing a day in your life? Pray about what you discover; ask God to show you any changes you need to make.

EMBRACING SOLITUDE

Everyone in the house is gone—for the entire weekend. How did those words make you feel? Were you considering who to call for a fun night out, or reveling in the thought of hours of uninterrupted quiet time to read, relax, and restore? Perhaps both ideas appeal to you: a little girl time, and a little alone time.

Jesus cherished his alone time. He guarded it. Amidst the stories of ministering to crowds, feeding thousands, and untold hours spent with the twelve he chose as apostles, it's easy to miss this fact. Studying the gospels, we see a pattern emerge: he healed, then he went off to pray alone; he taught, then he climbed the mountain to pray alone; the disciples went out on the boat, and Jesus remained on the shore—alone.

After sending them home, he went up into the hills by himself to pray. Night fell while he was there alone (Matthew 14:23, NLT).

Imagine Jesus slipping off, unnoticed, and going to spend time with his Father. What intimacy they must have shared; how restorative those hours of prayer must have been. Whatever your feelings about solitude, ask God to give you Jesus' heart for alone-time with him.

SEPTEMBER 10

SILENCE

If the radio were broken in your car, would you need to fix it immediately, or would you relish the silence? Perhaps you or someone you know keeps the TV on all day "for the noise." What is it about silence that makes so many of us uncomfortable? Some of us even talk to ourselves to avoid it.

Yesterday we explored solitude. Our feelings about silence often connect directly to our feelings about being alone. The radio keeps us from realizing we are alone, or from leaving us alone with our thoughts. But alone with our thoughts is exactly where God most wants to speak to us. How can we hear him if we're partially tuned to a song, show, or commercial? How can we listen if we never stop talking?

For God alone, O my soul, wait in silence,
for my hope is from him (Psalm 62:5, ESV*).*

Seek out silence today. Allow God to discern your needs, your questions, and then wait for him to answer.

FEAR

If you live in America, it is impossible not to look at today's date and remember—whether from experience or from hearing about it over the years—one of the darkest days in our history. Thousands of lives were lost in a well-planned terrorist attack, and in many ways, things were never again the same. Air travel, for example, continues to evoke a spirit of fear in many hearts that was previously unimagined.

In the New Living Translation alone, the word fear appears 601 times. Primarily, it is there to remind us to fear God; in doing so, he will abate all other fears. The fear God desires from us is not one of mistrust, but one of respect and awe. If we believe completely in his sovereign power, if we give him all our reverence, how *can* we fear anything else? If God is for us, there is truly nothing to fear. Hallelujah!

Fear and intimidation is a trap that holds you back.
But when you place your confidence in the Lord,
you will be seated in the high place (Proverbs 29:25, TPT*).*

What do you fear? Lay it at the feet of the Lord today, and place your trust in him. Know that no matter what your circumstances, your safety in him is secure.

JUST ASK HIM

Ah, the first crush. "Does he like me?" we wondered aloud to our friends. "Just ask him," they answered. "You may never know if you don't ask," they counseled. A note was written, folded, and passed. We waited nervously for the reply. The whole thing was simple, but also scary.

If only answers to prayer came so simply or quickly: "Should I take this job? Marry this man? Try to have a baby now, or in a year? Check yes or no." God's Word encourages us again and again to come to him with our questions, concerns, and deepest longings. He *does* promise a reply, though not necessarily in the form of a check in a box.

I call to you, God,
and you answer me.
Listen to me now,
and hear what I say (Psalm 17:6, NCV*).*

What are you longing to know? Just ask him. He's waiting expectantly for your prayers, and he will answer you. It may not be today, or even for a long time, but keep asking. Keep waiting for his reply. He hears you.

YOUR HEART'S DESIRE

What did you want more than anything else in the world when you were a little girl? Maybe having a pony or being a princess were the most delightful things you could imagine back then. What do you yearn for now? How different are your big-girl dreams?

We've all heard that God loves to answer our prayers and to grant our desires. Should we expect him, then, to give us whatever we want? Study the verse below, and notice in particular the first part. *When we delight in the Lord,* he gives us the desires of our heart. If we delight in financial success, washboard abs, or highly accomplished children, he makes no promises. This does not mean we are wrong for wanting these things, just that God isn't necessarily invested in making them happen for us.

> *Make God the utmost delight and pleasure of your life, and he will provide for you what you desire the most (Psalm 37:4,* TPT*).*

Take an honest look at the things you long for, dream about, and desire. What do they reveal about your relationship with God? What, if any changes do you need to make?

SEPTEMBER 14

FREE TO DO WHAT?

What would you do with a day of total freedom? All your obligations, limitations, and commitments are lifted. Do you head to a spa, shop 'til you drop, party like it's 1999? If we're being honest, most of us considered something along these lines.

Our challenge as daughters of the Almighty is to see freedom a different way. Paul admonishes the Galatians to look at the liberty they have because of Christ's sacrifice not as a license to indulge, but to reach out. Free of the restrictions of the Old Testament law, we needn't concern ourselves with having a clean slate, or making sure our neighbors do. We are free to meet the needs we see around us—to openly, freely love one another.

> *You, my brothers and sisters, were called to be free. But do not use your freedom to indulge the flesh; rather, serve one another humbly in love (Galatians 5:13,* NIV*).*

If you were to apply this concept of freedom to your own life, what might you do—where might you go? Search your heart for a way you long to serve others, and begin praying about how to make it happen.

SEPTEMBER 15

OUR DESTINY

As we listen to a talented singer, or watch a brilliant athlete, these people, so apparently effortless in their pursuits, seem born for just those things. This is their destiny, we think. *What is my destiny?* we may then wonder. *What was I born to do?*

Whether or not you believe you have a specific purpose, God knows you do. And he knows just what it is, and how long—how many false starts and poor decisions—it will take you to fulfill it. He is deeply interested in the destinies of those who call him Father, just as he is in the ultimate fate of the whole world.

> *These things I plan won't happen right away. Slowly, steadily, surely, the time approaches when the vision will be fulfilled. If it seems slow, do not despair, for these things will surely come to pass. Just be patient! They will not be overdue a single day!* (Habakkuk 2:3, TLB)

Are you waiting on God to fulfill—or reveal—your destiny? Take comfort in the passage above, and thank him for his perfect timing. If the waiting is hard, ask for his help.

NO MORE THIRST

Imagine a marathon with no water stops. A sideline with no giant cooler for the team. Immediately, we picture athletes dropping from dehydration and exhaustion. It's unthinkable.

What is the most thirsty you've ever been? How long had you gone without drinking, and how wonderful did those first few sips taste when your thirst was finally quenched? Perhaps one of Jesus' most audacious promises is to take away our thirst. It's extraordinary. He will be all we need, he tells us.

"Never again will they hunger;
never again will they thirst.
The sun will not beat down on them,"
nor any scorching heat.
For the Lamb at the center of the throne
will be their shepherd;
"he will lead them to springs of living water."
"And God will wipe away every tear from their eyes"
(Revelation 7:16-17, NIV).

Go back to your image of the marathon, and picture yourself running strong, completely free from thirst or pain. Ask the Holy Spirit to reveal what this might look like in your life today. What needs can Jesus meet? Thank God for the incredible promise of living water to come.

YOU ARE BEAUTIFUL

Stereotypes become stereotypes because of the truth in them. We think of a group of girls comparing flaws, calling themselves ugly while reassuring their friends of their beauty because we've seen it. We've heard it. We've lived it. Are you welcoming and accepting of the woman you see in the mirror, or do you analyze, criticize, and judge her?

Sisters, let us listen to what the Bridegroom says about us. Let us believe the encouraging words of others, and silence the voice in our heads that tells us we are anything but beautiful. The voice is a lie. God's Word is truth, and he says we are beautiful.

You are altogether beautiful, my darling;
there is no flaw in you (Song of Songs, 4:7 NIV).

Do you believe this? What would it take for you to see yourself as beautiful? Stand before your mirror—and smile. If this is difficult for you, ask Jesus, the Bridegroom, to show you what he sees.

SEPTEMBER 18

IN TIMES OF DOUBT

The sun will set tonight; it will rise tomorrow. This is truth. We have no reason to doubt what we've witnessed every day of our lives. But when experience tells us otherwise, or perhaps we have no experience to go on, doubts creep in. It's going to snow tomorrow. "I doubt that," we say.

When someone we trust says they'll be there for us, we have faith in their words. Someone who has repeatedly let us down can make the same promise, but we remain uncertain until they've shown up and proven themselves. We're unsettled. We doubt. God wants to erase our doubt and he will; we only need to have faith.

God you are near me always, so close to me;
every one of your commands reveals truth.
I've known all along how true and unchanging
is every word you speak, established forever!
(Psalm 119:151-152, TPT)

Examine your prayer life. Do you trust God, or do you doubt his promises to you? Why? Share your heart openly with him, and ask him for unwavering faith.

HE WILL GIVE YOU VICTORY

When we are little, an offense as small as borrowing a favorite pink marker without permission can create an enemy if only for an afternoon. We may even have sworn to hate the pretty little blonde chosen to play Cinderella.

As we grow, it takes a bit more. By the time we are women, for most of us, the concept of having an actual enemy is pretty foreign. That little girl, so incensed over the pink marker or Cinderella, is adorably amusing. We do have an enemy though, and he would like nothing more than to steal our joy and assure our defeat. His weapons? Jealousy, insecurity, and vanity, just to name a few.

> *"Listen to me, all you men of Israel! Do not be afraid as you go out to fight your enemies today! Do not lose heart or panic or tremble before them. For the LORD your God is going with you! He will fight for you against your enemies, and he will give you victory!" (Deuteronomy 20:3-4, NLT)*

What enemy are you fighting? Ask, and then allow God to fight for you, and be assured of your victory.

SEPTEMBER 20

TRUE HEALING

Examine your scars, and recall the wounds that gave them to you. Depending on the severity of the injury, and how long ago it occurred, running a finger along the scar may bring back vivid memories of the pain you felt. You are healed, but also changed.

Broken bones mend, but a limp or occasional twinge may remain. So might our fear; it can take a lifetime to fully trust our healing is complete—except for when God does the healing. When we ask God to remove old hurts, betrayals, and disappointments from our hearts, he removes them completely.

> *O Lord, if you heal me, I will be truly healed;*
> *if you save me, I will be truly saved.*
> *My praises are for you alone! (Jeremiah 17:14, NLT)*

It may be painful, but explore your old heart wounds, the ones that never seem to entirely heal. Begin today the process of releasing them to God, and claim the promise of his true healing.

SEPTEMBER 21

NOBODY'S PERFECT

Let's say you have a teenage daughter, and you're leaving her home alone. You trust her, but just so there are no misunderstandings, you leave her a list of no's: no parties, no boys in the house, no cooking with fire, no announcing on social media that you're home alone. Let's say she invites her boyfriend over. Even though she followed most of your instructions, she still broke the rules. Bring on the consequences.

God's law is no different, and that is why we need Jesus. Mess up one command? We've broken the rules. Bring on the consequences. Or…admit what he already knows. We aren't perfect. While we may never kill or steal or eat the wrong thing on the wrong day, we are entirely likely to covet, to take the easy way out, to gossip. Because of grace we get to choose: follow all the rules, or accept his forgiveness in advance.

Whoever keeps the whole law but fails in one point has become accountable for all of it (James 2:10, ESV).

What do you choose: your ability to keep every command, or God's grace? Spend some time thanking him for his incredible, undeserved gift of grace.

SEPTEMBER 22

RENEWAL

It's hard to find someone who doesn't love fall. The gorgeous colors; the return of scarves, sleeves, and cute boots; the peaceful silence of a home where kids have returned to their classrooms—all invite a spirit of renewal. As the outside air begins to change and leaves begin to fall, a clean slate seems entirely possible.

Even when life is humming along quite nicely, the idea of a fresh beginning is irresistible. For some of us, the transition from summer to fall feels more like New Year's Day than New Year's Day.

Teach me your ways, O Lord,
that I may live according to your truth!
Grant me purity of heart,
so that I may honor you (Psalm 86:11, NLT).

If God were to purify your heart, where would he begin? Spend some time dreaming with him about what this fall might bring to you, and what you might bring to it.

PLEASE REMAIN SEATED

When riding in a moving car, boat, or plane, we wouldn't just jump out, no matter how restless or impatient we were feeling. That would be crazy. We couldn't possibly expect to arrive at our destination as safely or as quickly—or perhaps at all. We grasp the necessity of remaining where we are if we are to get where we are going.

Why, then, are we so quick to jump ahead when it comes to God's plans for our lives? We accept his grace, but not his timing. We welcome his comfort, but not his discipline. How often do we decide without praying, or act without his prompting? And yet we expect to get where we are going—safely, quickly, easily.

> *"Remain in me, as I also remain in you. No branch can bear fruit by itself; it must remain in the vine. Neither can you bear fruit unless you remain in me"* (John 15:4, NIV).

Are there areas of your life you are trying to direct on your own? Spend some time praying for the Spirit to reveal to you anywhere you are not abiding in Jesus, or trusting his timing. Ask him to help you trust him.

NOT OUR POWER

We've all heard a story: a 110–pound mother stops a moving car with her bare hands, or defeats a charging bear, to save her toddler. We love the image of the tiny defeating the mighty. The sheer unlikeliness of it is what makes it so compelling; love will make the impossible, possible.

When we feel called to do something for God, our first instinct may be to list our shortcomings. We focus on *our* ability, *our* strength, forgetting the One who promises to equip us with all we need. We are like Esther, wondering, *What if I fail?* The fact we could easily fail is what makes it a great story.

> *We have this treasure in jars of clay to show that this all-surpassing power is from God and not from us (2 Corinthians 4:7,* NIV*).*

Have you felt God prompting you to do something that seems impossible? What if all you had to do was agree to try? Maybe you dream of accomplishing something but don't believe you could. What if he gave you that dream, and he's just waiting for you to ask for his help?

TRUST THE LIGHT

Imagine yourself in total darkness, perhaps a wilderness camping trip (or a power failure at a nice hotel if that's more your speed). It's the middle of the night, and you must find your way back to camp. Turn on your flashlight. Though it only illuminates a few steps at a time, it's enough to keep moving. Each step forward lights more of the way, and eventually, you see your destination.

Our faith walk is very much like this. Most of the time, we can't see where we're headed. Although just a few steps ahead is all we can make out for certain, we trust the path the light reveals.

> *"I am the Light of the world; he who follows Me will not walk in the darkness, but will have the Light of life" (John 8:12,* NASB*).*

Sisters, Jesus is our light. He shows us just what we need to see to put one foot forward at a time. Ask him to help you ignore the unseen and trust the light.

SEPTEMBER 26

WE LIVE BY FAITH

Yesterday, we pictured being led by a single beam of light, allowing its illumination to direct our steps. The flashlight helped us avoid a tangle of roots, or a dangerous drop-off. Take the journey a little deeper today, and imagine the batteries giving out. Once again, you're in darkness. What now? Cry for help. Ask someone who is already there to guide you.

Again, this is our faith walk. While Jesus' light never goes out, sometimes our sight does. We get so bogged down by circumstances, by sin, by our own agendas, we can't see a thing. So how do we keep moving? We cry out, and then we follow the sound of his voice. We must step more slowly now, but we can still walk. We just need to listen, and have faith in his voice.

In my distress I cried out to the LORD;
yes, I prayed to my God for help.
He led me to a place of safety;
he rescued me because he delights in me
(Psalm 18:6, 19 NLT).

Can you think of a time where you honestly couldn't see where you were headed? Perhaps that time is now. Are there steps you need to take in spite of your blindness to the path? Call out to him. Let his voice guide you home.

WHO ARE YOU TRYING TO PLEASE?

Think of a time you took a stand for your faith. Risking disapproval, you retained your purity despite pressure to "join this century." You confronted friends in the midst of a gossip session. You declined another invitation to an all-night wine party/husband-bashing session. Scary, wasn't it?

We want to be liked. God made us for community, so going against the community is hard. Most women crave harmony, so expressing an unpopular or "old-fashioned" opinion can be daunting. But what is the alternative? Think now of the last time you *didn't* take a stand for your faith. How did you feel afterward?

"Blessed are those who are persecuted
for righteousness' sake,
For theirs is the kingdom of heaven"
(Matthew 5:10, NKJV).

We were never promised this life would be easy. In fact, Scripture repeatedly points to the opposite. Resisting the world is hard; without the help of the Holy Spirit, it's actually impossible. Where do you need help living to please God and not people? Ask him to help you, and know that he will. And when you fail, know that he has *already* forgiven you.

SEPTEMBER 28

OUR COMFORTER

It's the end of a long, difficult day. All you want to do is crawl in bed, wrap up in your comforter, and rest. Something about a soft, fluffy blanket helps problems seem less like problems.

One of God's many names is the *God of all comfort.* He is our ultimate comforter, allowing us to wrap ourselves in him and be warmed, reassured, and relieved. He does this so we can pay it forward, wrapping ourselves around others in need of comfort, and showing them his love.

> *Praise be to the God and Father of our Lord Jesus Christ, the Father of compassion and the God of all comfort, who comforts us in all our troubles, so that we can comfort those in any trouble with the comfort we ourselves receive from God (2 Corinthians 1:3-4,* NIV*).*

Notice the repetition in the verses above. The word comfort appears four times. This isn't because Paul was feeling uninspired; it's because he wanted to make sure we heard him. We are comforted *so that* we can comfort. He wants both for us. Which have you done more of lately? Ask him to help you with the other.

DO EVERYTHING IN LOVE

What goes through your mind as you shop for groceries? How about during your workouts? While you read, or watch TV, do your thoughts turn to love? As you do dishes, is there love in the way you rinse a glass, or as you dry a pot?

First Corinthians contains the rather extraordinary command to do everything in love. Everything. What would that look like? How does one pick lovingly through packages of strawberries, searching for the reddest, juiciest ones? Is there a loving way to scrub the broiler pan? Perhaps not, but we most certainly can approach our daily lives in a state of love, filled with it, thereby assuring all we do will be done in love.

Do everything in love (1 Corinthians 16:14, NCV).

Rather than consider how to bring more love to your activities, pray today asking to be filled to the brim with love. From there, simply let it flow.

SEPTEMBER 30

FINDING PEACE

What does chaos look like in your world? Crazy work deadlines, over-scheduled activities, long to-do lists and short hours? All of the above? How about peace? What does that look like?

Most of us immediately picture having gotten away, whether to the master bathroom tub or a sunny beach. It's quiet. Serene. The trouble with that image, lovely as it is, is that it's fleeting. We can't live in our bathtubs or in Fiji, so our best bet is to seek out peace right in the middle of our chaos. Guess what? We can have it. Jesus promises peace to all who put him first.

You will keep in perfect peace
all who trust in you,
all whose thoughts are fixed on you! (Isaiah 26:3, NLT)

How appealing is it to imagine being unmoved by the stresses in your life? Is it easy or difficult for you to imagine claiming this promise for yourself? Ask Jesus to grant you true peace; fix your thoughts on him and watch the rest of the world fade away. When it tries to sneak back in, ask him again.

OCTOBER

Lord, you know and understand
all the hopes of the humble
and will hear their cries
and comfort their hearts,
helping them all!

Psalm 10:17 TPT

OCTOBER 1

SOURCE OF LIFE

There's a reason that the Bible refers to water hundreds of times. We have a continual thirst that needs to be satisfied. Our bodies themselves are made up of water! In fact, women's bodies are more than 50% water! Crops will not grow without water, and without them we'd have no sustenance. Water is the source of all life.

Jesus referred to himself as living water, and isn't it a fantastic analogy? When we have thirst for water, we drink, and it restores our bodies. And when we have a drought in our spiritual life, we need only seek him, and he will restore our soul. We never need to desire anything else but him because he will satisfy our spiritual dryness for our entire lives. We will never thirst again!

With joy you will draw water
from the wells of salvation (Isaiah 12:3, NIV*)*

Are you drinking from the cup that Jesus is offering you? Or are you searching out other things to dampen the drought in your life before you seek him? Everything needs water to survive, but God doesn't merely want survival for you. He wants to give you a supernatural quenching of the thirst in your life.

SLOW TO SPEAK

It's no secret; women love to talk. Get a bunch of women in one room, and there are times that you cannot hear yourself think over the sound of the chatter. We are often quick to cut in with a thought, because our minds race constantly with all that we have to say.

But nowhere in the Bible does it say, "You really should speak before thinking. Say what you want when you want to." Instead, it tells us to be quick to listen and *slow* to speak (see James 1:19). That's not an easy thing for us to do, especially when it seems we are built to talk!

Whoever guards his mouth and tongue
Keeps his soul from troubles (Proverbs 21:23, NKJV).

Listen for the word that the Lord himself has planted in you today. He wants to talk with you. Are you willing to listen? Take a moment to hear what he has for you.

OCTOBER 3

MIXED MESSAGES

Have you ever spent Sunday morning in a pew, proclaiming your love for God, then walked out and said to a friend, "Did you see Sally's skirt? It was *so* short!" Perhaps you judged as someone darted in fifteen minutes late to the service. Maybe you told yourself that you're a better person than Susie because Susie yells at her kids and you rarely yell at anybody.

If so, you're not alone. It's our natural tendency to put others down to make ourselves feel better. We hold the secret belief that if someone else looks bad, we'll look good by comparison. But the Bible tells us that we cannot praise Jesus and curse others at the same time.

> *With the tongue we praise our Lord and Father, and with it we curse human beings, who have been made in God's likeness. Out of the same mouth come praise and cursing. My brothers and sisters, this should not be. Can both fresh water and salt water flow from the same spring? My brothers and sisters, can a fig tree bear olives, or a grapevine bear figs? Neither can a salt spring produce fresh water (James 3:9-12,* NIV*)*

Keep careful watch over your thoughts and words today, being sure to lift others up as you climb closer to God.

LEAVES THAT NEVER WITHER

If you live in a cooler climate, then you've probably experienced the gorgeous season that is fall. Each year, the leaves slowly turn to shades of golden yellow, orange, and red. It's a thing of beauty, but eventually, the leaves wither and die, then fall to the ground.

All too often, the same can happen with our relationship with the Lord. We get that initial fire for him; we burn brightly with it, but lose our way and fall away from him. If we keep our trust in him, he tells us that our spiritual leaves will never wither. He wants our lives to be like trees that continually bear fruit.

"It does not fear when heat comes;
its leaves are always green.
It has no worries in a year of drought
and never fails to bear fruit" (Jeremiah 17:8, NIV).

Are you bearing good fruit in your spiritual walk, or have you begun to fall away? Plant your roots deeply in him, and let him water your soul.

OCTOBER 5

WHERE CREDIT IS DUE

You achieve a goal, or you get some wonderful news. The day you've been waiting for has arrived, and you're so excited about it. What is your first reaction? Do you update your status on social media to let your friends know what you've done? Do you call up your mom and tell her the wonderful news?

There's nothing wrong with sharing your excitement with others. But when doing so, be sure to first give the glory and praise to God. He has given you everything you have. Get excited about how good he has been to you. When you're just so happy that you can't help but dance for joy, be sure to give Jesus a twirl too. He wants to celebrate with you!

"Give praise to the Lord, proclaim his name;
make known among the nations what he has done,
and proclaim that his name is exalted.
Sing to the Lord, for he has done glorious things;
let this be known to all the world" (Isaiah 12:4-5, NIV).

Are you giving credit where it's due? Be sure to take some time today to thank the Lord for all that he has helped you achieve, and for all that he has given you. He wants to share in your excitement!

SEEING THE GOOD

Are you a glass-half-full person, or do you live your life looking for the next tragedy to strike? It can be tempting to dismiss the good we see in our lives because we're too busy being on the lookout for the negative.

God wants to honor those who are obedient to him, and sometimes his blessings are so good they're almost unbelievable. Even Abraham, so blessed by God that he was chosen to father a nation, laughed when God gave him good news.

> *"As for Sarai your wife, you are no longer to call her Sarai; her name will be Sarah. I will bless her and will surely give you a son by her. I will bless her so that she will be the mother of nations; kings of peoples will come from her." Abraham fell facedown; he laughed and said to himself, "Will a son be born to a man a hundred years old? Will Sarah bear a child at the age of ninety?" (Genesis 17:15-17,* NIV*)*

Look past the pain, the hurt, the trouble in your life. Can you spot the good? Don't laugh it off! Rejoice in your blessings today.

OCTOBER 7

MY WAY

Most women have a stubborn streak, and we come by it honestly. We've spent so much time caring for others that we have learned to do it incredibly well. To put it plainly, we just don't want anybody else telling us how to do something because we know we can do it better.

Because of this, it can be really difficult to let go of our own way of doing things and release our lives to God. This will only backfire on us in the long run. The Bible tells us that if we are guided by the Spirit, we will live in peace. The other option? Death.

> *The mind governed by the flesh is death, but the mind governed by the Spirit is life and peace. The mind governed by the flesh is hostile to God; it does not submit to God's law, nor can it do so. Those who are in the realm of the flesh cannot please God (Romans 8:6-8,* NIV*).*

Submit your life to what he has for you. Pray for a spirit of obedience. You may be fabulous at what you do on your own, but God has even greater things in store for you if you'll only give him a chance.

PRAY LIKE YOU MEAN IT!

When you pray, are you doing it in a spirit of boldness, or are you praying weak prayers? It's as if we are afraid to bother God with our requests. For goodness sake, we better not pester him too much, or perhaps he won't answer them at all, right? So we speak tentatively, "Dear Lord, if it is your will, it'd be great if you could..." "Father, I know you have so much on your plate, but I'd love it if...."

Let's stop with the weak prayers. You're not a wimp; you're a woman! The Lord knows your heart already. Believe that he can do what you are asking. There is no need for caution with the Father who loves you so dearly. Jesus said so himself.

> *"'If you can'?" said Jesus. "Everything is possible for one who believes." Immediately the boy's father exclaimed, "I do believe; help me overcome my unbelief!" (Mark 9:23-24,* NIV*).*

Step out boldly in faith, beginning with your prayer life. Are you talking to God in a spirit of timidity? Ask him for help in overcoming your disbelief. Everything is possible for those that believe, so set your heart upon doing so.

THE GAME OF OPINIONS

As soon as you accepted Christ as your Savior, you were welcomed into a special group. As Christians, we are called to live a life set apart because our actions should reflect Christ himself. But all too often, we get caught up in a game of opinions, and we begin bickering amongst ourselves about right and wrong.

Whether the topic is what women should wear, or how we should vote, or even whether to vaccinate, people have strong opinions. And heaven forbid anyone should have an opposing one! If you've ever read the comments section on any online article or social media posting, then you've seen how ugly it can get, and how quickly. So what happened to peace? When did we stop showing each other our love?

> *As a prisoner for the Lord, then, I urge you to live a life worthy of the calling you have received. Be completely humble and gentle; be patient, bearing with one another in love. Make every effort to keep the unity of the Spirit through the bond of peace (Ephesians 4:1-3,* NIV*).*

Are you living a life that is worthy of the calling you received as a Christian? Pray for a spirit of love and peace today.

RULED WITH GRACE

God's law was given so that people could see how sinful they were. But instead, we began to sin more and more. You'd think God would've given up on us, but instead, he gave us grace in abundance. We make terrible decision after terrible decision, and still he loves us and shows his mercy.

Though we deserve to be punished for our faults, God rules with his wonderful grace. Jesus died so that we would be given the gift of eternal life in heaven. Think of all the sacrifices you make for others, and then consider what it would take to sacrifice *yourself* so that others could live. Talk about the gift of a lifetime!

> *The law was brought in so that the trespass might increase. But where sin increased, grace increased all the more, so that, just as sin reigned in death, so also grace might reign through righteousness to bring eternal life through Jesus Christ our Lord (Romans 5:20-21, NIV).*

Spend some time thanking the Lord for the great gift he has given you today. Whereas once we might've lived under the law alone, now we live in grace and mercy. Let us not forget the sacrifice he made for us.

OCTOBER 11

WEARY TO THE CORE

Have you ever been run so ragged that you just didn't know if you could take even one more step? Your calendar is a blur of scheduled activities, your days are full, your every hour is blocked off for this or that, and it's hard to find even a spare minute for yourself. Even your very bones feel weary, and you fall into your bed at night, drained from it all.

There is someone who is ready to catch you when you fall. You might stumble throughout your busy day, but he will never let you hit the floor as you take a tumble. God delights in you! He will direct your every step if you ask him to. He will gladly take you by the hand and guide you.

The steps of the God-pursuing ones
follow firmly in the footsteps of the Lord.
And God delights in every step they take to follow him.
If they stumble badly they will still survive,
for the Lord lifts them up with his hands
(Psalm 37:23-24, TPT*).*

Are you allowing the Lord to guide your days? Though you may be weary, he has enough energy to get you through it all. Hold out your hand to him today and walk side-by-side with Jesus.

OCTOBER 12

IS IT RELEVANT NOW?

Sometimes it can feel as though the Bible doesn't really speak to our modern lives. After all, these stories took place thousands of years ago. It doesn't always seem relevant. Old Testament people lived for hundreds of years. We can't fathom being swallowed by a fish when we try to avoid God's presence. Rainbows are beautiful, but it's hard to picture the entire earth being covered in water, so we forget that rainbows are a symbol of his covenant with us.

There is truth woven throughout every word in Scripture, and there is much to relate to as women! Deborah was an amazing leader. Ruth and Naomi show a picture of friendship and love. Mary Magdalene went through struggles and was healed. Esther was incredibly brave.

> *The word of God is alive and active. Sharper than any double-edged sword, it penetrates even to dividing soul and spirit, joints and marrow; it judges the thoughts and attitudes of the heart (Hebrews 4:12,* NIV*).*

The Word of God is alive today and just as relevant as it was for the original readers. Love, joy, peace, patience, kindness, goodness, faithfulness, gentleness, and self-control—these attributes are waiting for you if you dive in and seek it out.

OCTOBER 13

HIDDEN BLESSINGS

There are hidden blessings to be found in the midst of our troubles. One of them is that we are better able to care for others and to show compassion when we have been there ourselves. God is the source of all comfort, and he teaches us this gift as well.

The Lord shows us mercy and gives us peace that passes understanding even in the middle of our greatest pain. Because of this, when others are troubled and struggling, we have learned the true meaning of comfort and we're able to pass it along.

"They are blessed who grieve,
for God will comfort them" (Matthew 5:4, NCV).

Do you know someone who is going through some sort of battle? Think back to the ways our Father reached out to you during your time of pain. Use that knowledge to bring comfort to your friend. Who better to learn from than God himself?

EVERY PART WORKING TOGETHER

The Bible tells us that God knit us together in our mothers' wombs. Before we were born, our bodies were carefully selected and created by our Maker, ensuring that each part worked with the others to function on the whole. Great care was put into this process.

As Christians, we are all a part of the body of Christ. Just like our physical bodies, if each part is working together with the others, then the entire body functions well and is happy. But if just one part is suffering, the entire body suffers.

> *God has put the body together, giving greater honor to the parts that lacked it, so that there should be no division in the body, but that its parts should have equal concern for each other. If one part suffers, every part suffers with it; if one part is honored, every part rejoices with it.*
> *Now you are the body of Christ, and each one of you is a part of it. (2 Corinthians 12:24-27,* NIV*)*

What care are you taking to be sure that the body of Christ, your community of believers, is working together? Are you rejoicing together? Look for ways in which you can contribute to the harmony of the body around you.

OCTOBER 15

FLIP THE SWITCH

Have you ever walked through your home at night, thinking that you could make it without turning a light on, only to stumble on something unexpectedly set in your path? When you cannot see where you are going, you are likely to get tripped up. On the other hand, your way is obvious when you simply turn on a light.

The Bible tells us that walking in righteousness is just like walking in the bright light of day. But choosing rebellion is like stumbling around in a deep darkness. You never know what hit you until it's already too late.

The lovers of God walk on the highway of light,
and their way shines brighter and brighter
until they bring forth the perfect day.
But the wicked walk in thick darkness,
like those who travel in a fog
and yet don't have a clue why they keep stumbling!
(Proverbs 4:18-19, TPT)

Are you choosing the light? Is your path brightly lit? Or are you standing in total darkness? If so, then flip the switch! Pray that you will make wise choices. Seek his wisdom for your life! He wants to shine brightly for you. Let him in, and he will gladly be your eternal light, illuminating your days.

OCTOBER 16

CHOOSING WISDOM

The word *wisdom* is used hundreds of times in the Bible. Time and time again, we are instructed to use good judgement, to make sound decisions, to use prudence and circumspection. King Solomon made a special point to ask God to give him wisdom throughout his time as Israel's leader. Because of this, God honored and blessed him.

The interesting thing is that wisdom is often referred to in Scripture as a "she." Since the beginning of time, God has known that women are capable of making wise decisions. In Proverbs, she beseeches us to find her, to choose her. She tells us that if we do, we will find favor with God.

If you wait at wisdom's doorway,
longing to hear a word for every day,
joy will break forth within you as you listen for what I'll say.
For the fountain of life pours into you every time that you find me,
and this is the secret of growing in the delight
and the favor of the Lord (Proverbs 8:34-36, TPT).

Are you choosing wisdom? Are you seeking her out? Spend some time at her doorway today. True happiness is found there, and the Lord will honor your decision!

OCTOBER 17

BUILDING YOUR HOUSE

Building a house can be really fun for some and really stressful for others. There's so much to choose, and so many details to go over. Color schemes, cabinet choices, carpeting, and... the list goes on and on. It can be overwhelming for some.

But building your spiritual house is easy. The only thing you need to worry about is choosing the right foundation. Jesus himself gives us his instructions on how to do so.

> *"Everyone who hears these words of mine and puts them into practice is like a wise man who built his house on the rock. The rain came down, the streams rose, and the winds blew and beat against that house; yet it did not fall, because it had its foundation on the rock. But everyone who hears these words of mine and does not put them into practice is like a foolish man who built his house on sand. The rain came down, the streams rose, and the winds blew and beat against that house, and it fell with a great crash" (Matthew 7:24-27,* NIV*).*

Are you building your spiritual house on a solid foundation? Listen for his words, and put them into practice in your daily living.

OCTOBER 18

FINDING LOVE

You're telling a really good story, one you believe to be true, when suddenly, someone calls you out. "Liar!" they say. Taken aback, you look at them as if they are crazy. You know what you're saying is the truth. How could they accuse you of telling false tales?

The harsh reality is that if we have hardness in our hearts toward a fellow believer, we cannot truly claim to love God. *Ouch.* He told us to love our neighbors as ourselves. He calls us to be as one with the body of Christ. Yet, we often find fault with our brothers and sisters in the church—to the point where we can't find love for them at all. It's not what he wants for us.

> *Whoever claims to love God yet hates a brother or sister is a liar. For whoever does not love their brother and sister, whom they have seen, cannot love God, whom they have not seen (1 John 4:20,* NIV*).*

If there is someone within your community of believers whom you struggle to love, pray that the Lord will give you the supernatural power to do so. It's only through him that we can find the strength to love those that we couldn't otherwise.

OCTOBER 19

LIGHTHOUSES

There's a good reason why lighthouses were built. For hundreds of years, they've shined brightly across harbors around the world, guiding ships safely to shore. The premise was simple; put the light up high where it can easily be seen.

Jesus is the light of the world. That light wasn't meant to be hidden away. It's meant to be put up high, where everyone can easily see it. And as his followers, we are called to shine brightly for him, in such a way that others can see it for themselves. We don't hide it away; we boldly light the way to Christ.

> *"You are the light of the world. A town built on a hill cannot be hidden. Neither do people light a lamp and put it under a bowl. Instead they put it on its stand, and it gives light to everyone in the house" (Matthew 5:14-15,* NIV*)*

Don't keep your light for Christ hidden away, bringing it out only when it feels comfortable. Pray that you will have the boldness of faith to be a source of light for everyone with whom you come in contact. Ask the Lord to help you shine brightly so that others may step out of the darkness and join you in the light.

CHOOSE OBEDIENCE

The Word of God is pretty clear. Though we often want to ignore it, or walk away for a while, if we are seeking his wisdom, then there is no getting around the fact that we need to choose obedience. The Bible tells us over and over that we are to keep his commands. If we do so, we will find blessings in our lives. If not, life looks pretty bleak.

It's not always easy to choose a life of obedience. Our fleshly desires spring up constantly, getting in the way of what we are called to do. But in the long run, walking with the Lord is a life filled with joy. Our earthly possessions and ambitions will only leave us feeling flat.

> *I command you today to love the Lord your God, to walk in obedience to him, and to keep his commands, decrees and laws; then you will live and increase, and the Lord your God will bless you in the land you are entering to possess (Deuteronomy 30:16, NIV)*

Pray for a spirit of obedience so that God can increase his blessings in your life. Walk side by side with him today, seeking his will.

OCTOBER 21

NEW LIFE

Have you ever laid in bed at night, thinking over past wrongdoings and beating yourself up over decisions you made years ago? If so, you are not alone. Women can be incredibly hard on themselves, asking for near perfection.

There is good news for us all! Once we accept Christ as our Savior, we are made new. There is no need to continue to berate ourselves for the choices of the past. He has washed away our sins and made us clean. We don't have to look at life from our former point of view because our old lives are gone and new ones have begun!

> *The LORD is good to all, and his mercy is over all that he has made (Psalm 145:9, ESV)*

Release your past to the Lord. If you struggle to get past a mistake you once made, ask him for help in forgiving yourself. You have been made new in the eyes of the Lord! There is so much freedom in this knowledge! Enjoy it!

LOSING TO GAIN

The key to growing in your faith is simple. There must be less of *us* in order to have more of God. To allow more of his presence into our lives, we must give up more of ourselves. We need to place our lives before him as an offering and give him our all.

The world would say that giving up ourselves is a loss. We've been taught for years that we must put ourselves first. Our fellow man would say that we need to make ourselves a priority. But oh, are they missing out! When we give ourselves over completely to God, we get to share in his glory and in his great joy. Setting aside our earthly pleasures for heavenly treasures means we gain a lot more than what this world could ever offer us.

> *"If you try to hang on to your life, you will lose it. But if you give up your life for my sake, you will save it" (Matthew 16:25, NLT).*

Empty yourself of the desires of your flesh and allow God to fill you with his presence. You won't feel a lack. In fact, it will overflow in your life, spilling out everywhere for others to see! Become less, so that you can gain more of him.

OCTOBER 23

IN SUNSHINE AND STORM

It's easy to feel happy on a sunny day, when all is well, the birds are singing, and life is going along swimmingly. But what happens when waters are rougher, bad news comes, or the days feel just plain hard?

God wants us to feel gladness when times are good. He has made each and every day. We are called to rejoice in all of them whether good or bad. Happiness is determined by our circumstances, but true joy comes when we can find the silver linings, hidden in our darkest hours—when we can sing his praises no matter what. We don't know what the future holds for us here on earth, but we can find our delight in the knowledge that our eternity is set in beauty.

When times are good, be happy;
but when times are bad, consider this:
God has made the one as well as the other.
Therefore, no one can discover
anything about their future (Ecclesiastes 7:14, NIV).

Is your happiness determined by your circumstance? Pray that you will discover true joy in our Creator. Ask him to give you a deep and abiding satisfaction in each day that goes beyond human understanding.

A LIFE OF WORSHIP

When we are truly diving deep into a growing relationship with God, our entire lives become a living, breathing act of worship.

The sacrifices you make, like when you wake up early to spend time with him instead of hitting snooze one more time, or when you give up a night at home to attend an evening of prayer at your church, are examples of this kind of worship. When you take your ordinary moments and you give them up to God, they become forms of devotion to him.

> *I ask you from my heart to give your bodies to God because of His loving-kindness to us. Let your bodies be a living and holy gift given to God. He is pleased with this kind of gift. This is the true worship that you should give Him. (Romans 12:1, NLV –need new version)*

Take your everyday moments, whether sleeping, eating, going to work, or just walking around, and give them over to God in the spirit of worship today. Let your entire being be a song of praise to your Savior!

OCTOBER 25

POWER WITHOUT LIMIT

There is only so much that we can accomplish in our own strength. We plow through our tasks, and we can get a lot done. But we are limited in our power.

God has no limit in what he can do! If we ask him to work in our lives, there's no stopping the amazing things that will happen! We can accomplish more than we'd ever think to ask for. The best part is that he *wants* to do it for us. It's not a chore for him or another task to cross off his list so that you'll stop pestering him.

> *To him who is able to do immeasurably more than all we ask or imagine, according to his power that is at work within us, to him be glory in the church and in Christ Jesus throughout all generations, for ever and ever! Amen (Ephesians 3:20-21, NIV).*

Ask the Lord for bigger and bolder things. Pray that he will give you the supernatural ability you need to accomplish all that's before you. His power is without limits, and he will extend it to you if you'll only ask him for it!

OCTOBER 26

TRUE RICHES

Once you've experienced the true beauty of a relationship with Christ, everything else becomes somehow insignificant. What you once held dear no longer seems important.

Compared to knowing Christ as your Savior, everything else the world values just pales in comparison.

> *Whatever were gains to me I now consider loss for the sake of Christ. What is more, I consider everything a loss because of the surpassing worth of knowing Christ Jesus my Lord, for whose sake I have lost all things. I consider them garbage, that I may gain Christ and be found in him, not having a righteousness of my own that comes from the law, but that which is through faithfulness in Christ—the righteousness that comes from God on the basis of faith. I want to know Christ—yes, to know the power of his resurrection and participation in his sufferings, becoming like him in his death, and so, somehow, attaining to the resurrection from the dead (Philippians 3:7-11,* NIV*).*

Have you fully embraced the ways of God? Would you be willing to lose everything for him? Grasp a hold of the beauty he's offering. Pray for a heart that's glad to be rid of earthly treasures and eager for what's in store for a true believer.

OCTOBER 27

OVERCOME THE OBSTACLES

Life on planet Earth is not always an easy one. In fact, we will go through many times of trouble. Perhaps you are in the middle of a struggle right this very moment! Cheer up; God has an amazing message of hope that he wants you to hear.

We have been created in his image. We are called to live a life modeled after Jesus. He tells us that he has already overcome the world. That means we are overcomers! We can take this world and all its heartaches and pain by storm. And we have the biggest cheerleader standing by our side the entire time—our Lord and Savior!

"I have told you these things, so that in me you may have peace. In this world you will have trouble. But take heart! I have overcome the world" (John 16:33, NIV*).*

When we rely on the world to bring us joy, we find only temporary happiness. But in him, we find peace. Trust him, so that you may have an unshakeable assurance that you can overcome the obstacles that have been placed in your path today.

IN THIS TOGETHER

We can often find ourselves seeing all the ways in which we are different. You take your coffee black, and your friend takes hers with more cream than caffeine. You vote one way, your neighbor votes another. Maggie is an introvert, and Melanie won't stop talking.

But here's the thing we have in common: no matter who we are or what we believe, Jesus Christ died for us all. Each and every one of us falls into the category of "all." There's nobody left out. He died for Maggie, he died for Melanie, and he died for your neighbor who votes differently than you do. One man died for everyone, and this puts us all on the same page.

> *Christ's love compels us, because we are convinced that one died for all, and therefore all died. And he died for all, that those who live should no longer live for themselves but for him who died for them and was raised again (2 Corinthians 5:14-15,* NIV*).*

Look for the similarities between you and those around you. Are you praying that you can break down walls and stand on the truth? We are all in this together!

OCTOBER 29

BOLD AND CONFIDENT

Each and every day, we are given the most incredible opportunity. We are given the chance to talk to a God who has been in our shoes. A *man* who literally walked the walk. He is waiting for us to walk up to him and ask him anything.

Jesus went through the same things we do during his time on earth, so he truly understands where we're coming from when we approach him. We don't need to muster up our courage! He wants us to be confident. Esther was bold when she approached her king about saving her people, and that guy was known to make rash and terrible decisions! We get to talk to a King who is known for his mercy.

> *My voice You shall hear in the morning, O Lord;*
> *In the morning I will direct it to You,*
> *And I will look up (Psalm 5:3,* NKJV*).*

Are you holding back tentatively in your time with your heavenly King? Be bold, and be confident! He loves you. He understands you. He wants the best for you. He will show you grace and mercy in whatever it is that you seek.

DANCE UNHINDERED

Peer pressure is real, even for adults. We often worry about how we will look in the eyes of others. *Do I look okay today?* we wonder. *I forgot to bring the garbage can in. What will the neighbors think?* we ask ourselves.

There was at least one person who didn't care what others thought of him. King David was so excited after winning a big battle that he went whooping and dancing, praising God as he marched home to his family. When his wife scorned him for looking foolish, he had no time for her words.

> *"It was before the Lord, who chose me rather than your father or anyone from his house when he appointed me ruler over the Lord's people Israel—I will celebrate before the Lord. I will become even more undignified than this, and I will be humiliated in my own eyes. But by these slave girls you spoke of, I will be held in honor"* (2 Samuel 6:21-22, NIV).

Are you worried about what others think, or are you concerned with what God thinks of you? Dance in God's presence today, no matter what you may look like! He wants to celebrate life with you.

OCTOBER 31

EYE ON YOU

Did you know that long before you decided to take the plunge and accept Christ into your heart as your Savior, he had his eye on you? He was waiting for you to come to him so that he could share with you his eternal gift. God wanted glorious living for you. And oh, how he celebrated when you made that decision!

It is through Christ that we discover who we are. When we put our hope in him, we find ourselves. It's in him that we learn what we are living for. And he works all of our lives together as Christians for the greater good.

> *In him we were also chosen, having been predestined according to the plan of him who works out everything in conformity with the purpose of his will, in order that we, who were the first to put our hope in Christ, might be for the praise of his glory (Ephesians 1:11-12,* NIV*).*

You were chosen by God. He waited for you, and he rejoiced when you came to him. Celebrate with him today! Praise him for the gift he has given you in eternal salvation. He is so good!

So be truly glad. There is wonderful joy ahead, even though you have to endure many trials for a little while. You love him even though you have never seen him. Though you do not see him now, you trust him; and you rejoice with a glorious, inexpressible joy.

1 Peter 1:6, 8 NLT

NOVEMBER 1

TRUTH ABOUT LEGALISM

When we buy into the lie that how we live our earthly lives determines whether or not we will have eternal life, we lose sight of the entire point of the Gospel. *Legalism* is the term for believing that doing good works will make you right with God. But the people in the Bible who dedicated their lives to "doing the right thing" (the Pharisees) are the very same people who put Jesus on the cross.

Legalism isn't a holier form of God-worship; it's self-worship. When we give ourselves a role in our own salvation, we are claiming to be able to do something only Jesus is capable of. The grace of Christ alone is what saves us.

> *The love of God is this, that we obey his commandments. And his commandments are not burdensome (1 John 5:3, NRSV).*

Your obedience doesn't carry the weight of your righteousness. You have righteousness through faith in the Son of God. You have only to love him. In your love, you will desire to obey him because you know that obedience will bring you closer to him.

THE WRITING ON THE WALL

What types of messages do we allow to enter our homes on a daily basis through television, social media, internet, magazines, smartphones, or even our own conversations? Do we take the time to really ponder and evaluate the ideas that we absorb even sub-consciously?

Let the messages in your home be messages of godliness. Let your loved ones see and hear the words of life and truth above those of sin and death. Choose carefully the words and images that enter your home and your heart.

I will be careful to live an innocent life.
When will you come to me?
I will live an innocent life in my house.
I will not look at anything wicked.
I hate those who turn against you;
they will not be found near me.
Let those who want to do wrong stay away from me;
I will have nothing to do with evil (Psalm 101:2-4, NCV).

The Holy Spirit will be your greatest ally when determining which messages you should or should not allow into your home. Listen to his prompting, and don't ignore him when he gently tells you that something isn't healthy for your spirit. Print some of your favorite verses out and hang them on your walls.

NOVEMBER 3

BELIEVE HE IS GOOD

The first sin ever was committed by a woman. Eve, the mother of all, changed humanity forever when she made one fatal decision to venture outside God's boundaries. When Eve took a bite of the fruit, she did more than just give in to her own desire for pleasure, she opened the door of sin to every generation that would follow after her.

Eve's key mistake was that she doubted the goodness of God. The serpent knew he could penetrate a woman's mind with well-spoken words, and he convinced Eve that God was withholding something from her. As she believed that God was depriving her, she also believed that God wasn't good after all—that he didn't have her best interest at heart. The moment Eve stopped believing God was good was the moment that temptation overcame her.

Adam was not the one deceived; it was the woman who was deceived and became a sinner (1 Timothy 2:14, NIV).

How often do you doubt the goodness of God? Do you wonder if the boundaries he's put in place are really necessary or right? Do you doubt that God really cares about the details of your life? Remember that God *is* good, and that you can trust him completely.

OUR BEAUTIFUL GIRLHOOD

Close your eyes for a moment and think back to when you were a little girl. Do you see her? What is she like? Excitable? Passionate? Quiet? Shy? Remember for a moment what it was like to be that little girl: caring nothing of dirty hands or mussed-up hair. Caring only for that moment—the fleeting moment of freedom and unpredictability. A girl who can lose herself in make believe and dreams. A girl who knows how to dance wildly and run freely. A girl who knows full well the arts of day dreaming and wild flower picking.

That little girl grew up quickly, didn't she? Responsibility eventually overtakes carefree spontaneity. Reality drowns out limitless dreams. Restoration of full well-being can be ours! Doesn't that sound just like childhood? Beloved, God can restore to you what's been lost.

Let their flesh be renewed like a child's;
let them be restored as in the days of their youth'—
then that person can pray to God and find favor with him,
they will see God's face and shout for joy;
he will restore them to full well-being (Job 33:25-26, NIV).

What life has threatened to strip from you, God can restore and reshape. Forget today about the things which never really mattered all that much, and remember what it is to breathe life in your lungs.

NOVEMBER 5

WE HAVE TIME

Time is one of those things we never seem to have enough of. Many of our days can feel like a race against the clock to get everything done. We seem to lack the time we need for even the most important things—things like being in God's Word, spending intentional time with loved ones, or volunteering to help those in need.

At the end of the day, there is one reality we must remember: we have time for what we make time for. It's easy to feel busy, but what are we truly busying ourselves with? Are we finding time to spend browsing social media or watching re-runs of our favorite TV shows? Are we finding time to take a long shower or sleep for a few extra minutes in the morning? None of those things are necessarily *wrong*, but if we feel pressed for time and unable to spend time with the Lord, we may need to rethink where our time goes.

> *Be careful how you live. Don't live like fools, but like those who are wise. Make the most of every opportunity in these evil days. Don't act thoughtlessly, but understand what the Lord wants you to do (Ephesians 5:15-17,* NLT*).*

Take a good hard look at your day today and think about how you can spend your time most wisely—in a way that will make the most of the moments and opportunities you have.

NOVEMBER 6

THE BURNING BUSH

Do you ever feel like your life is in a holding pattern? Like your *something big* must be lurking around the next corner. You may feel like your life is being wasted while you wait for your own destiny.

God had Moses in a very similar holding pattern. He had this incredible experience at birth where he was specifically saved from certain death, miraculously found by the most powerful woman in the land, and raised as royalty. He had an unbelievable launch to his life, and then, after a fatal mistake, he became your average sheep herder in the desert for the next forty years. *Forty years.* That's a long time to wonder if the greatness of the vision you were born into will ever come to fruition.

The most amazing part of Moses' story, is that after all the waiting, God came to him in one of the most famous ways in history—and we all know how incredibly God went on to use Moses after that.

> *"When forty years had passed, an Angel of the Lord appeared to him in a flame of fire in a bush, in the wilderness of Mount Sinai"* (Acts 7:30, NKJV).

Remember, if you feel directionless right now—without vision and without destiny—know that no wilderness is too remote for you to stumble upon a burning bush. You have only to trust, to watch, and to wait.

HUMILITY

God values humility over pride and earthly success. That is why sometimes God makes us wait before revealing his plans for us. In the waiting is where he grows us in humility. When things don't work out perfectly, our pride is dismantled and we learn the most valuable lessons.

God being glorified in our lives doesn't make sense to our humanity because his plan isn't our plan and his ways are different. The entire message of the Gospel is upside-down from what we know here on earth. In God's kingdom, humility is elevated and pride is made low. Those who are poor are rich, and those who are weak are strong.

> *Humility is the fear of the* LORD;
> *its wages are riches and honor and life* (Proverbs 22:4, NIV).

God is more concerned with having your heart fully devoted to him than he is with you having a successful ministry. He wants you to serve him, and he loves when you prosper in kingdom work, but those things aren't his main goal. His main goal is to be with you forever. Humble yourself in his presence today.

TRUE RELIGION

Many people today ask what religion can do for them. How can it alleviate their fears, save them from death, and improve their quality of life? Christianity has never been about what we can get from it.

True religion— the kind that is acceptable to God—is found in giving ourselves to those who need the most. It's not about our comfort, our happiness, or even our ticket to heaven. It's about reflecting the glory of Christ on the earth.

Pure and undefiled religion in the sight of our God and Father is this: to visit orphans and widows in their distress, and to keep oneself unstained by the world (James 1:27, NASB).

The tender Father heart of God is far more interested in developing your love and Christ-like character than he is in keeping you comfortable. His compassion and intense love for mankind will not be satisfied with comfortable, cushioned Christianity. If you want to bring praise to God, intentionally seek out situations where you can put into practice your undefiled religion. Make it your mission to meet needs, to love, and to bring life.

NOVEMBER 9

THE COST OF SACRIFICE

What are you not doing right now because of fear? Are there things you are keeping quiet about simply because you're afraid? Are there steps forward that you aren't taking because you're frightened about what may happen if you do? Are there stirrings in your heart that you're neglecting because you're afraid of how you may be criticized?

In the Bible, when God announced what he was about to do in someone's life, he often began it with the words, "Do not fear." He knew we would worry. He knew we would list the cons and stress over the details, and he said *don't.*

> *However, the king said to Araunah, "No, but I will surely buy it from you for a price, for I will not offer burnt offerings to the Lord my God which cost me nothing." So David bought the threshing floor and the oxen for fifty shekels of silver (2 Samuel 24:24,* NASB*).*

Jesus died on the cross and paid the price for our *lives*—not for our money or our talents. He doesn't just want the parts that others see. He wants the secret, hidden parts of us. What are you holding back from God? In light of what his death cost him, is there really a price too high for your sacrifice to him?

NOVEMBER 10

A "YES" FAITH

Have you ever stepped out and said yes to something crazy for God? You followed him into the middle of the ocean and trusted him to keep you afloat. Stepping out in faith isn't easy. In fact, it's messy. It's a lot of wondering what you're doing, and why you're doing it. It's a lot of closing your eyes and begging God to remind you of all the things he placed on your heart when he originally gave you the vision. When you stand in the truth that you have obeyed, it doesn't really matter how everything looks or feels. What matters is that you were obedient. You believed what God was telling you.

Stepping out in faith is about boldly facing your harshest critics and telling them you're not sure if everything will work out. It's being at peace in total chaos. It's putting yourself out there and wondering if you'll live up to expectation. It's wondering if you have anything to offer after all.

> *Abram believed the Lord. And the Lord accepted Abram's faith, and that faith made him right with God (Genesis 15:6, NCV).*

There is peace in obedience—peace that even when you're criticized, laughed at, and misunderstood, the God of the universe is pleased. And everything else fades away in light of that awesome reality. If God is asking you to do something that terrifies you, step out in faith. Obey him. Believe him. It will be worth it.

NOVEMBER 11

STORYTELLING

We enjoy listening to stories because they help us to relate with a concept and personalize an idea. We hear a lofty explanation and struggle to understand, but a story illustrates the same thought and we become connected to it.

Jesus was a storyteller. While he walked the earth, he told people many stories in order to teach them something. Jesus used parables and imagery instead of "just spitting it out" so that people would meditate, speculate, study, and absorb the words to better understand them. The parables that Jesus told weren't just simple stories; their symbolisms revealed secrets of the kingdom of heaven and made its glory digestible for the common man.

> *Jesus constantly used these illustrations when speaking to the crowds. In fact, because the prophets said that he would use so many, he never spoke to them without at least one illustration. For it had been prophesied, "I will talk in parables; I will explain mysteries hidden since the beginning of time" (Matthew 13:34-35,* TLB*).*

When people who don't know God hear the Gospel, it can be confusing because their eyes have not been opened by the Holy Spirit. When you share with them your own story of God's work in your life, their hearts and minds may be more easily opened.

NOVEMBER 12

APPETITE

Appetite is a funny thing. Our bodies have the ability to communicate hunger to our brains, and our brains then cause us to seek out a solution to the problem. When we are genuinely hungry, we look for food that will fill our stomachs and quiet our hunger.

Our souls have appetites also, but we so easily fill our time and energy with the world's entertainment. We fill ourselves up with things that will never be able to satisfy and leave little room for the only one who can.

> *No one can serve two masters; for a slave will either hate the one and love the other, or be devoted to the one and despise the other. You cannot serve God and wealth (Matthew 6:24,* NRSV*).*

There is a throne in your heart upon which only one master can sit—and you must choose wisely who will take residence there. Will you allow your life to be ruled by the pursuit of things which will never last, or will you accept nothing less than eternal stock for your life's investment?

NOVEMBER 13

CONTINUAL PRAISE

It's relatively easy to sing God's praises when all is going well in our lives: when he blesses us with something we asked for, when he heals us, or when he directly answers a prayer. We naturally turn and give him praise and glory for *good* things. What about when things aren't going well? What about in dry times, painful times, or times of waiting?

Do we only praise God for something after he's given it, or do we praise him ahead of time in faith, knowing that he will always be good no matter what happens? We should look at all difficulties in life as miracles waiting to happen—chances for God to show his goodness and bring us closer to his heart.

I will praise the Lord at all times;
his praise is always on my lips (Psalm 34:1, NCV*).*

Choose today to have praise readily on your lips instead of complaint. Whenever you feel discontentment or frustration, replace it with praise. By focusing on the goodness of God, the hardships will lessen and your joy will increase.

A LOVE THAT IS FELT

Think about the most romantic movie you've ever seen. Two beautiful people portray an even more beautiful love on the silver screen, taking your heart on a romantic adventure as they play out passion right before your eyes. But behind the camera, do those two people really feel that love? They are *actors*. They are good at what they do. They can make that love story look so very real.

Is love really love when given outwardly but not felt inwardly? Even though it may look to everyone around you that you are passionately in love, if that love is not genuine in your heart, then it's not love at all.

> *"These people come near to me with their mouth*
> *and honor me with their lips,*
> *but their hearts are far from me.*
> *Their worship of me*
> *is based on merely human rules they have been taught"*
> *(Isaiah 29:13,* NIV*).*

If our worship is borne out of true love and intimacy, it will go much further than the outward displays of affection. Our love will permeate our hearts and our lives. We will not just *look* like someone in love, we will *be* in love.

NOVEMBER 15

A WARM WELCOME

Have you ever met someone and immediately felt a connection? Maybe you were drawn to their personality and a friendship was born. Have you ever met someone you struggled to connect with? Maybe the way they dressed, acted, talked, or chose their career was completely foreign to you.

We all have our natural friendships. We don't have to be best friends with everyone we meet because the truth of it is, we won't. But what if, despite our differences, we still accepted all those we come in contact with?

Accept one another, then, just as Christ accepted you, in order to bring praise to God (Romans 15:7, NIV).

As Christians, our main goal is to bring praise to God. By accepting others with the same measure of absolute acceptance that Christ extends to us, we honor God and bring him praise. Let's strive today to accept those around us and to genuinely welcome them with open arms in spite of our differences.

EMOTIONS

It is no secret that women can be emotional. We are complicated creatures who feel deeply. Sometimes our emotions make us feel like a bit of a mess, so we try to hide them from those around us—and even from God.

God created us to live with a full range of emotions. He is aware how those feelings directly impact our daily lives. God is not frustrated with us as we feel all of the things that he created us to feel. He is not offended by our anger, impatient with our tears, or bothered by our laughter.

Is anyone among you suffering? Let him pray. Is anyone cheerful? Let him sing praise (James 5:13, ESV).

Don't be tempted to come to God with your emotions covered up. Allow him to see your raw emotion in all its honesty. Lay everything before him, holding nothing back. He loves you and he will stick with you through good times and bad.

NOVEMBER 17

NO CONDEMNATION

Most of us know the story of the woman caught in adultery. One of the intriguing moments was when Jesus was questioned about whether or not the woman should be stoned. His response is to stoop down and start writing in the dirt. Jesus' action of stooping in the dirt literally defines one interpretation of the word *grace*.

As they all stood casting judgement, Jesus removed himself from the accusers, stooping low and occupying himself elsewhere. It spoke volumes about his lack of participation in the crowd's judgement. Because of Jesus' distraction, the eyes of the onlookers were drawn off the woman, perhaps lifting a portion of her shame. With their attention focused on Jesus, he said the words that saved the woman's life: "Let him who has never sinned cast the first stone." One by one, the accusers walked away.

> *Straightening up, Jesus said to her, "Woman, where are they? Did no one condemn you?" She said, "No one, Lord." And Jesus said, "I do not condemn you either. Go. From now on sin no more" (John 8:10-11,* NASB*).*

Jesus was the only one qualified to stone the adulterous woman. This is a beautiful foreshadowing of the redemption he later brought to all sinners. Beloved, Jesus is the only one qualified to condemn you, and he chose to condemn himself instead. You are free and clean because of the grace of Jesus Christ.

NOVEMBER 18

PERSEVERANCE

Do you remember when you first decided to follow Christ? Maybe you felt like a huge weight was being lifted off you, or that the peace and joy you'd been searching for was finally yours. You were filled with excitement in your newfound life, and you felt ready to take on the world in the name of Jesus.

Following God may come easy at first. We accept him into our lives and are swept into his love with incredible hope. But as time goes on, old temptations return, and threaten to shake our resolve. The confidence we felt in our relationship at first lessens as we wonder if we have what it takes to stick it out in this Christian life.

> *Do not throw away this confident trust in the Lord. Remember the great reward it brings you! Patient endurance is what you need now, so that you will continue to do God's will. Then you will receive all that he has promised (Hebrews 10:35-36, NLT).*

Perhaps you have lost the confidence you had at first. Or maybe you are still in that place of complete confidence and trust. Either way, step boldly forward into all that God has for you. Remain confident in him; he will accomplish what he has promised. When following him gets hard, press in even harder and remember that you will be richly rewarded for your perseverance.

NOVEMBER 19

PERFECT LOVE

Does anyone know the *real* you? The you that hasn't been edited or exaggerated?

Putting up a false front in our relationships is a direct expression of our own fear. When we are afraid to be truly known, we lose out on the most incredible gift that can be given in relationship—honest love. We sacrifice genuine relationship on the altar of our own insecurity and fear.

> *We know the love that God has for us, and we trust that love. God is love. Those who live in love live in God, and God lives in them. This is how love is made perfect in us: that we can be without fear on the day God judges us, because in this world we are like him (1 John 4:16-17, NCV).*

Are you afraid to be fully known? Lay down your need to be perceived as perfect, and allow yourself to be loved for who you truly are. Let your fear be washed away by the perfect love of a perfect God.

SANCTUARY

Since sin entered the world in the Garden of Eden there has been a divide between the holy God and humanity. But throughout history, God has created ways for us to still have fellowship with him despite the separation that sin caused.

God wants to be with us. He didn't shrug his shoulders when sin entered the world and reconcile himself to the fact that he wouldn't be able to have a close relationship with us any longer. No, rather, he went to the greatest lengths to still be with us because his love for us is that intense. God wants to dwell among us. Not just visit. Not just talk sometimes. He wants his presence to be constantly among us.

Let them make Me a sanctuary, that I may dwell among them (Exodus 25:8, NKJV).

Are you creating a sanctuary in your life where God can dwell? Are you fostering an atmosphere that will welcome the holy God? He longs to be near you.

NOVEMBER 21

MONEY TROUBLE

Sometimes money can feel like water in our hands. It slips right through our fingers, and is gone as soon as it's acquired.

As Christians, we know that we should trust God with our every need. But do we really? Are we confident that no matter what circumstances come our way, God is going to take care of our finances? Or do we become consumed with worry that we will not have enough? Right after God tells us not to love money, he reminds us that he'll never leave or forsake us. He knew that we would worry about our finances. He knew that fear would come far more easily than contentment.

> *Keep your lives free from the love of money, and be content with what you have; for he has said, "I will never leave you or forsake you" (Hebrews 13:5,* NRSV*).*

Remember that no matter how little or how much money you have, God is control. He is more than able to provide for all your needs and he will never forsake you.

NOVEMBER 22

THE RIGHT REST

As women we tend to be expert multitaskers. We juggle many responsibilities, schedules, and details. As the holiday season approaches, these tasks only seem to increase. Between the cooking and decorating, the parties and festivities—we can easily get tired out.

God says in his Word, "Be still and know that I am God." He asks us to stop, to sit, and rest because he designed us to *need* rest. There is a reason God set the example by resting on the seventh day after he made the world. Even the Creator knew the importance of rest.

"My Presence will go with you, and I will give you rest" (Exodus 33:14, NIV*).*

Have you ever gotten up from the couch and still felt weary—sometimes even wearier than when you sat down? Don't confuse resting your body with resting your soul. True life-giving rest comes only from being in the presence of the Father. Pause within the busyness of the impending holiday season to sit before God, read his Word, and wait on him as you recharge in his presence.

NOVEMBER 23

THIRST FOR PURE WATER

Have you ever noticed that the more consistently you drink water, the more your body thirsts for it? And the less you drink water, the less you consciously desire it. Though you still need water to live, you become satisfied with small amounts of it disguised in other foods and drinks. But for a body that has become accustomed to pure water on a daily basis, only straight water will quench its thirst.

The same principle applies to God's presence in our lives. The more we enter his presence, the more we long to stay there. The more we sit at his feet and listen to what he has to say, the more we need his Word to continue living. But if we allow ourselves to become satisfied with candy-coated truth and second hand revelation, we will slowly begin to lose our hunger for the pure, untainted presence of the living God.

I want more than anything
to be in the courtyards of the LORD's Temple.
My whole being wants
to be with the living God (Psalm 84:2, NCV).

Does your entire being long to be with God? Press into Jesus until you no longer can be satisfied with anything less than the purest form of his presence. Cultivate your hunger and your fascination with him until you literally crave him. Spend your life feasting on his truth, knowing his character, and adoring his heart.

PREPARED TO SERVE

A natural response to feeling the love of God is to want to do things for him. But we have to become people of God before we can effectively do God's work. The only way to become his people is to spend time in his presence.

The disciples didn't go directly from responding to God's call to full time, full blown ministry. They spent a lot of time with Jesus first—learning from him, talking with him, and watching him minister.

> *"Very truly, I tell you, the Son can do nothing on his own, but only what he sees the Father doing; for whatever the Father does, the Son does likewise. The Father loves the Son and shows him all that he himself is doing; and he will show him greater works than these, so that you will be astonished" (John 5:19-20,* NRSV*).*

Not even Jesus acted without first paying attention to what God was saying. Take time to be quiet before God and ponder his words and his plans. Through knowing his heart, you will discover where he is already working and you will be able to join him in his will.

NOVEMBER 25

GIVING THANKS

What happens in our souls when we say *thank you* to God? When we consecrate a passing second by breathing gratitude into it? What happens to our very being when we acknowledge the weight and glory of even the most insignificant gift?

With each moment of paused reflection, each thank-filled statement, we are set free. Set free from negativity. Set free from dark thoughts of death, pain, suffering, and ugliness. We enter *his* gates with thanksgiving. We enter his holy place. We walk directly through the door he created.

Swing wide, you gates of righteousness,
and let me pass through,
and I will enter into your presence to worship only you!
I have found the gateway to God,
the pathway to his presence for all his lovers
(Psalm 118:19-20, TPT).

To walk in thanksgiving is to walk right into God's presence. This season of thanksgiving has a way of taking our hearts and righting them. It opens our eyes to wonder and splendor in casual moments. It puts things into perspective and restores triumph to the defeated soul. Practice saying thank you today—knowing that through your thankfulness, you will usher yourself into the presence of God.

REJOICE, PRAY, THANK

It is easy for us to get weighed down with the negative things in this world. Our lives, and the lives of those around us, are full of troubles that make us weary. Some days it can be difficult to find joy in the midst of our own chaos.

We wonder what God's will is, especially in the hardships. We can't see his master plan, but feel as though if we could, maybe we could make it through. We wonder what God wants us to do in the midst of our difficulties.

> *Rejoice always; pray without ceasing; in everything give thanks; for this is God's will for you in Christ Jesus (1 Thessalonians 5:16-18,* NASB*).*

These three things: constant rejoicing, prayer, and thanksgiving are the formula for doing God's will in our lives. Throughout the day, think about what you're thankful for. Rejoice continually in what God has done for you. Thank God intentionally for those things.

NOVEMBER 27

LAMB OF GOD

When we step into the holy presence of God, our sin becomes obvious. We feel the separation and shame that our mistakes have built. There is nothing we can do to eliminate our sin and restore our connection to the living God. We need a solution and we have none.

When Adam & Eve sinned and discovered their nakedness, God killed a young lamb and clothed them with it. In this action, God set the monumental precedent that the blood of an innocent lamb covers sin. The blood of the Lamb, Jesus Christ, would be shed on the cross centuries later to cover the sin of all mankind.

> *The next day he saw Jesus coming toward him and declared, "Here is the Lamb of God who takes away the sin of the world!" (John 1:29,* NRSV*)*

Nothing is hidden from God's sight. He knows your sin, he knows your shame, and he knows your predicament. But he made the sacrifice demanded for your sin. Jesus shed his own blood, and that blood covers your sin. All of your shame, all of your error, all of your unworthiness is erased by the work he already did. Rest in his unfailing love for you and in his power to take away your sin.

NOVEMBER 28

PERFECT

Each of us is keenly aware of our own weaknesses. We know all of our flaws too well and we make eliminating them our goal. But no matter how much effort we put out, we can never and will never achieve perfection.

Despite most of us realizing that we will never be perfect, we still put unreasonable pressure on ourselves. Whether in a task, in our character, or in our walk with Christ, we easily become frustrated when we reach for perfection and can't grasp it. But if we allow perfectionism to drive our performance, then we will quench our own potential and inhibit our effectiveness.

> *His divine power has granted to us everything pertaining to life and godliness, through the true knowledge of Him who called us by His own glory and excellence (2 Peter 1:3, NASB).*

God gives you the freedom to not be perfect. In fact, his power is all the more perfect when displayed in your weakness because when you aren't the main point, Jesus is. When you mess up, God has to take over and the result of that action is always perfection.

NOVEMBER 29

STILLNESS

Dusk settles on a chilly winter night. A gray fog hovers and snow begins to fall: cold, blustering snow…the kind that sticks. The snow keeps coming until you can barely see one hundred feet in front of you. In the woods it's quiet; all you can hear is the gentle wind, and all you can see is snow and trees. A pure white blanket of snow restores the earth, and as it falls, it restores you.

Sometimes we have to get outside of the noise and chaos of our own four walls. We have to step out into the snow, or the sun, or the breeze. We have to get alone, get silent, and clear the clutter from our minds and hearts as we stand in God's natural sanctuary.

Be still, and know that I am God;
I will be exalted among the nations,
I will be exalted in the earth! (Psalm 46:10, NKJV*)*

There is so much power in the stillness of knowing God as you stand serene in the world he created. The busyness of your life will always be there, but never forget to take the moments you can, to stop and know your God. In those moments you will find refreshment and strength to take on whatever will come next.

IT'S A WONDERFUL LIFE

Have you ever seen the holiday movie *It's a Wonderful Life?* It's an old classic, and it's easy to see why when you watch it. The feelings of the actors onscreen are so pure and raw—and utterly relatable. We have a lot of nights similar to those in the movie: nights where everything goes wrong and we ask, "Why?"

There are so many things in our lives that we simply don't get. We aren't sure why some things happen and other things don't. We have our own lofty dreams and treasured plans, and when they don't work out the way they did in our hearts, we feel lost, angry, and confused.

A man's heart plans his way,
But the LORD directs his steps (Proverbs 16:9, NKJV).

When everything goes wrong and the plans in our hearts don't work out, God knows what he's doing. He sees what we do not. We can have the best ideas in the world, but if God is not directing us, our plans will falter. Trust in him with all of your heart. Dedicate your plans to him, and allow him to make you his perfect masterpiece.

Whatever is good and perfect comes down to us from God our Father, who created all the lights in the heavens. He never changes or casts a shifting shadow.

JAMES 1:17 NLT

DECEMBER 1

THE TABLE

The Christmas season is like no other. You're invited to Christmas parties where you get to dress up and make your favorite appetizer. You can snuggle up on the couch and drink hot chocolate while watching old classics as your Christmas tree lights twinkle behind you. You can get together with girlfriends who are in different stages of life and have a memorable night of laughter and fun. The season feels almost magical.

One of the best areas to experience this time of year is around the table. Something beautiful happens when friends and family gather around delicious food. Conversation can lead almost anywhere. The beauty of the Christmas season is discovered in smiles, laughter, and joy-filled memories.

> *There were shepherds living out in the fields nearby, keeping watch over their flocks at night. An angel of the Lord appeared to them, and the glory of the Lord shone around them…I bring you good news that will cause great joy for all the people. Today in the town of David a Savior has been born to you; he is the Messiah, the Lord. This will be a sign to you: You will find a baby wrapped in cloths and lying in a manger (Luke 2:8-12, NIV).*

In this season, is there a time you can gather loved ones together and have a laughter-filled evening?

DECEMBER 2

THE TWINKLING LIGHTS OF CHRISTMAS

Have you ever turned into your neighborhood during this time of year and felt transported to another place entirely? Christmas lights are up, transforming ordinary homes into a magical world of twinkling, beautiful colors. Through the windows of your neighbors' homes you see trees, decorated with ornaments and bulbs. Santa figurines are creatively displayed on rooftops and reindeer are intentionally placed throughout the yard. At this time of year home feels even more special. More beautiful. More of a blessing.

If you don't have lights on your own house, enjoy the scene around you. Take time to drive around and reflect on the reason these houses are transformed. The birth of Jesus is a beautiful reminder of the gift of salvation, and this season is a perfect reason to reflect on that in the silence of twinkling lights and illuminated Christmas trees.

> *"No one lights a lamp and hides it in a clay jar or puts it under a bed. Instead, they put it on a stand, so that those who come in can see the light" (Luke 8:16,* NIV*).*

What does this season mean to you amidst the lights and transformation?

THE STORYTELLER

Going to the mailbox at this time of year is an exciting adventure. You never know what you're going to get. When you open the mailbox and see all those white envelopes holding Christmas cards, it's thrilling to rip them open, gaze at the pictures, and read the letters. Some families write pages, updating you on every family member and road trip taken. Some friends have a picture with a simple *Have a very merry Christmas*, and others will ride along the middle with a picture and a quick update. Each of these tells a story.

We *all* have a story to tell: a creative, intricate story designed just for us by the one who determines our steps. It does not matter if your card has a single picture of just you, or you with a husband, or you with a husband and five kids. It does not matter if your card has a picture of your apartment, your dream home, your convertible, or your minivan. It is a story that is beautifully yours and one that should be nourished and nurtured every step of the way.

Let the redeemed of the LORD tell their story (Psalm 107:2, NIV).

Your story changes as you do. Pray that as it does, you keep your eyes on the Storyteller. Reflect on your current story for a few minutes. What is your prayer as you continue on your journey?

DECEMBER 4

OUR FATHER IN HEAVEN

Do we know in the depths of our hearts that our prayers are heard: both the shouting cries for help and the gentle whispers of thanksgiving? He knows our every thought before we even think it. This is the Father that created us and calls us by name. We are his beloved daughters.

Believe it, beautiful women. We need to let the truth sink into the very deepest parts of our hearts and rest there in thanksgiving. His Word is truth, and he tells us time and time again that he will answer our prayer because we trust in him (see 1 Chronicles 5:20). Whether through song, action, thought, or speech, he delights in hearing our prayers.

The Lord sees all we do;
he watches over his friends day and night.
His godly ones receive the answers they seek
whenever they cry out to him (Psalm 34:15, TPT).

Do you take time daily to pray to your loving Father? If not, start the practice of talking with him in the car, in the shower, or sitting in silence in your room. What you say doesn't have to be fancy or long; God just desires your conversation and communion with him.

INSATIABLE GOD

Jesus died on the cross to set us free. He suffered, he wept, he bled, he endured. Forever. For our freedom. What are we doing with that freedom? Are we continually playing it safe? Are we doing all we can to cast aside our fleshly desires and focus on the one great prize? How do we spend our time and energy?

Let's pray that we desire less of the world and more of Christ. Let's pray that we see our freedom for what it is. Let's pray for worldly desires to dissipate and hearts that cultivate courage to stand for what is good and right.

I will tell of the kindnesses of the Lord,
the deeds for which he is to be praised,
according to all the Lord has done for us…
according to his compassion and many kindnesses
(Isaiah 63:7, NIV).

How can you stop focusing on stuff and instead focus on furthering his kingdom? This is not an easy task in today's world. Gather some thoughts and meditate on what it looks like for your life.

DECEMBER 6

BALANCE BEAM

Have you ever taken an exercise or dance class where balance is a crucial component? Or gone for a run and knew that finding a comfortable pace was the only way you were going to complete the run?

As women, we have a lot of responsibility. Whatever season of life we are in, we most likely wear a hat that fits somewhere into the category of entrepreneur, scheduler, baker, driver, chef, employee, sister, daughter, friend, wife, or mother. You might wear only one hat, but most likely, you're juggling multiple hats a day. This can be a blessing, but it can also feel like a weight. Finding balance amidst the busyness of life is crucial to your hat fitting comfortably.

> *Seek first the kingdom of God and his righteousness, and all these things will be added to you (Matthew 6:33,* ESV*).*

What can you change about your day today to give you more balance? Think about a meeting you could shorten so you can take a quick walk, or inviting a friend to lunch, or skipping the gym and going to a coffee shop for an hour to read. Find the balance that makes you a better you.

DECEMBER 7

CHRISTMAS GIFT

The Christmas season is one of love. It is a season of remembering that the God of the universe came down to earth as a babe, changing everything. It is a season of longing with the adventure of Advent. It is a testament of celebration.

Trees. Twinkling lights. Comfy jammies. Warm tea. Friends. Family. Traditions. Delicious food. Presents. Thoughtfulness. Comfort. Joy. Beauty. Salvation…in the form of a baby.

The Christmas season is one of salvation. It is a beginning to be cherished and devoured at the same time. With abandon, recognize the gift of Jesus and what it meant for God to send him down to save us. He truly is the best gift of all.

> *"She will give birth to a son, and you are to give him the name Jesus, because he will save his people from their sins" (Matthew 1:21, NIV).*

In the busyness of this Christmas season, stop and remember what it is all for. We are a saved people. Thank you, Jesus.

DECEMBER 8

MYSTERY AND HOPE

There is so much mystery to life. So many unanswered questions and unknowns. Faith in and of itself is a huge element of mystery. In order to live a faith-filled life, we accept the elements of mystery because we know what goes hand-in-hand with it…hope. Hope is God telling us that his purpose is bigger than any unknown. When we walk through anything, no matter how great a mystery, God is walking alongside us.

God doesn't promise us an explanation, and therein lies the mystery. But he does promise his presence, and that is an unfailing truth. When we walk through deep waters, he is there.

> *Since through God's mercy we have this ministry, we do not lose heart. Rather, we have renounced secret and shameful ways; we do not use deception, nor do we distort the word of God. On the contrary, by setting forth the truth plainly we commend ourselves to everyone's conscience in the sight of God…For God, who said, "Let light shine out of darkness," made his light shine in our hearts to give us the light of the knowledge of God's glory displayed in the face of Christ (2 Corinthians 4:1-2, 6, NIV).*

Have you had a moment of mystery? An unexplained circumstance or situation that you wish you could ask God about? Know deep in your heart that hope is waiting on the other end of the mystery.

AFTER THE HEART

There is a difference in maturity of faith when we start to see God as our Father instead of just our Creator. We start to discern his voice amidst all the other voices, and we recognize that our actions, thoughts, and lack of trust can leave him yearning for us to be back in his grasp.

As much as we might feel there are other people God desires more or is more proud of because of their spiritual maturity, it is a lie. Sweet daughters of the one true King, he pursues our hearts with abandon. He desires our love. He yearns for the times we speak to him.

> *You have not received a spirit of slavery leading to fear again, but you have received a spirit of adoption as sons by which we cry out, "Abba! Father!" (Romans 8:15, NASB)*

Do you know that God pursues you? Let that thought permeate your being. He—the Creator of the universe, Abba Father, Alpha and Omega, I AM—pursues *you*. He longs for you to know him. Wherever you are on your spiritual walk, be encouraged that he will not stop pursuing you.

DECEMBER 10

JOURNEY OF THE WISE MEN

In the Bible, the wise men traveled a great distance to find the Savior. They were armed with gifts, and when they found him, they presented those gifts in honor of him. Can you even imagine what that must have been like? Knowing you were staring at the Savior of the world as a tiny baby, and trying to digest what his presence would mean to the world? It's incredible.

This time of year, what can we do to honor him? How can we be his hands in helping others? The Christmas season is a great time to engage in something unique because there are usually a lot of great opportunities. How can you spread his love in a different way?

> *When they saw the star, they were filled with joy! They entered the house and saw the child with his mother, Mary, and they bowed down and worshiped him. Then they opened their treasure chests and gave him gifts of gold, frankincense, and myrrh (Matthew 2:10-11,* NLT*).*

How could you spread the love of Jesus this Christmas season? Is there something you've been wanting to do but haven't yet? This might be the perfect opportunity.

DECEMBER 11

THE GOOD FIGHT

God has asked us to join him in the fight for his kingdom. In order to feel confident in what that looks like, we need to understand that having courage is God-given. Having courage to fight for our Father, to fight for our brothers and sisters, is given through the Spirit of God. The same Spirit that lives in him is alive in us—that thought alone must push us.

Second Timothy promises us that our spirit gives us power, love, and self-discipline. In order to see the fullness of God's Spirit, we need to take a step. It doesn't need to be a full-blown jump—just a single step to ignite a flame. A step might be taking a colleague to coffee, asking your waiter if they belong to a church, or reaching out to that neighbor you've always wondered about.

> *I remind you to fan into flame the gift of God, which is in you…for the Spirit God gave us does not make us timid, but gives us power, love and self-discipline…join with me in suffering for the gospel, by the power of God (2 Timothy 1:6-8, NIV).*

A step is powerful; it can plant a seed the size of a mustard seed. And that same mustard seed can move a mountain, further his kingdom, and glorify his purpose. What does stepping out and joining the fight look like for you?

DECEMBER 12

GEMS

When you sign up for a competitive team sport, you have a basic understanding that you're going to have to work hard and that emotions will run high to win and succeed. You know that you'll win some, you'll lose some, and that somewhere along the way you'll start to feel good about playing the game whether you win or lose.

Playing a competitive team sport can sometimes feel the same as building relationships with other women. We win some—forming incredible relationships—and others we lose. We were created uniquely, and while we are asked to love one another, it doesn't mean that we hope for a best-friend relationship with each woman we meet.

When we do find those friends, those precious few who make us better people by encouraging us and making us laugh, we need to hold on tight and enjoy the rare gems they are.

Sweet friendships refresh the soul
and awaken our hearts with joy,
for good friends are like the anointing oil
that yields the fragrant incense of God's presence
(Proverbs 27:9, TPT*).*

Do you have a friend that holds you accountable but also lifts you up when you need it? Share how much she means to you today. If you're still looking for a close friend, don't lose heart. Pray for God to bring just the right woman into your life.

HERO

When Jesus came down from sitting at the right hand of the Father as the Savior of the world, it was a rescue mission. He came down, in love, and rescued us. He delivered us from our sin.

We are forever his. And we are forever freed. There is no other love that loves without borders. And it is free. Let that resonate in your heart. He came down in love and rescued you…for free.

Jesus truly is the hero in our fairy tale. No matter what we experience today, we should let that sink in.

> *Grace to you and peace from God our Father and the Lord Jesus Christ, who gave Himself for our sins so that He might rescue us from this present evil age, according to the will of our God and Father, to whom be the glory forevermore (Galatians 1:3-5,* NIV*).*

Have you ever doubted God's love for you? Reread this and let the truth of it sink deep into your heart. You have been rescued, and his love for you is without boundary.

DECEMBER 14

LOVE WELL

If we do anything right, let it be that we love well. Loving well looks different for each person, but we know it when we do it: when we love whole-heartedly. We can't change the entire world—only Jesus can do that—but we can change the world for one person.

There are big things you can do to love well, but loving well can be done in little, everyday moments too. We love despite feelings. We love when it's tough. We love when we don't necessarily want to. We love well because we are called to: because God loved us first.

> *Follow God's example, therefore, as dearly loved children and walk in the way of love, just as Christ loved us and gave himself up for us as a fragrant offering and sacrifice to God (Ephesians 5:1-2,* NIV*).*

In what ways can you love well? Are there some you don't feel you love well that you can aim higher for? Ask God to help you love the way he does. Ask him to give you his heart for those he has placed in your life.

THE CALL FOR HELP

Depending on the type of person you are, you may not be very good at asking for help. There are those who like to be the *helpers*: they do best serving others because they feel capable and useful. Then there are those who gladly accept service any time they are given the opportunity. Neither is better than the other, and both have their positive elements.

In different seasons of life, natural helpers may need to be the ones receiving help. Sometimes this is hard to accept, and we have to be careful not to let pride take control. Asking for help is part of being vulnerable: we push everything aside to say, "I can't do this alone." God has put people in our lives who love to help, but they won't know we need it until we ask.

I look up to the hills,
but where does my help come from?
My help comes from the Lord,
who made heaven and earth (Psalm 121:1-2, NCV).

Can you easily ask for help? God asks you to take a chance on the people he's intricately placed in your life. You'll be amazed at how much stronger you feel when you're leaning on those who want to carry the load with you.

DECEMBER 16

CHEER FOR THE PRIZE

Have you ever watched cheerleaders at a sporting event? Smiling, bubbly, energetic, yelling for their beloved team. What we don't see is what might be going on underneath all of that encouragement. Everyone has their issues. And yet there they are, faithfully devoted to their team because they know the prize at the end.

In this same way, let us encourage one another in our faith. Imagine our Abba Father's joy when he sees us lifting each other up in praise and loving despite whatever we might have going on. There is so much to be gained in relationship with other believers whether on the receiving or giving end. And the prize at the end is eternity. There is nothing greater.

> *May the God who gives endurance and encouragement give you the same attitude of mind toward each other that Christ Jesus had (Romans 15:5,* NIV*).*

What are some ways you can encourage others? Think of the delight in God's heart when he sees you giving your time and talents.

CLAY

Life can be busy. Whatever season you are in, there are always things to be done. More often times than not, our wellbeing is cast aside because of all the other things that need to be tended to. Our Creator says that we are jars of clay. If left out and not tended to, that jar of clay can dry out and crack.

If we can give God our obedience and our time, he promises us his abundance and peace, quenching our very driest parts. Oh, daughters, the renewal we receive when we sit in his presence, letting him fill our spirit with his love and gentle, encouraging words!

Now, O Lord, you are our Father;
we are the clay, and you are our potter;
we are all the work of your hand (Isaiah 64:8, ESV).

When do you feel most renewed? Wherever you are right now in your walk, God hears your cries for renewal, your whispers of longing for his peace to fill your soul. Take time today to be refreshed by his Word and sit with him in prayer.

DECEMBER 18

LET GOD WIN

Don't believe the lies. There is an enemy out there who wants to steal, kill, and destroy. One of the most powerful ways he does that is through filling our hearts with things we think are true about ourselves. Those lies fill our minds with hatred, so that when we look in the mirror, we start hating what we see. *I'm so ugly. I don't deserve anything good in my life. I screwed up again; why do I even try?*

These thoughts make the Father weep. Beloved daughters, he loves us! He knits us together and sets us apart. He cherishes every breath we take, and in the name of Jesus, we can rebuke the enemy so those lies no longer fill our heads and overtake our hearts.

> *Truthful words stand the test of time,*
> *but lies are soon exposed (Proverbs 12:19,* NLT*).*

What are the lies that tear you down? Ask Jesus to lift the veil from your eyes so you can see clearly. You serve a God who would move mountains for you, a Father who loves his daughter more than anything else, and a Creator who delights in seeing you smile.

CYCLE

Have you ever said or done something that you immediately regretted? It just happened: that horrible moment that we replay over and over again. Then, maybe a few days later, something similar happens. Why does this happen? Why can't we exercise more self-control?

Those moments are the vicious cycle of our humanness. Thankfully, through the blood of Jesus Christ and our repentance, we are forgiven, set free, and released of the burden of our mistakes. We are given a clean slate to start over. And some days that gift feels bigger than others. Some days we rely heavily on the grace of our Lord and Savior just to get through the day. And that is okay.

> *To the praise of the glory of His grace, which He freely bestowed on us in the Beloved. In Him we have redemption through His blood, the forgiveness of our trespasses, according to the riches of His grace which He lavished on us (Ephesians 1:6-8, NASB).*

Have you had a "moment" recently? Do you know you are forgiven through the blood of Jesus? Accept his gift; you are forgiven. Forgive yourself and keep moving forward.

DECEMBER 20

DO YOU REALLY NEED IT?

Christmastime is a wonderful time, full of celebration and goodwill. So it seems right to get into the spirit of Christmas and gift-giving. Most of us love the opportunity to shop until late, buy good gifts for our friends and family, and maybe even splurge a little on ourselves.

Generosity is a wonderful thing to exhibit during the Christmas season, but let's not confuse giving with spending.

> *Tell those who are rich not to be proud and not to trust in their money, which will soon be gone, but their pride and trust should be in the living God who always richly gives us all we need for our enjoyment. Tell them to use their money to do good. They should be rich in good works and should give happily to those in need, always being ready to share with others whatever God has given them (1 Timothy 6:17-18, TLB).*

Have you fallen into the trap of thinking that spending will give you enjoyment? The Scripture says that God is the source for our enjoyment. He would rather we use our money to do good. Gifts are wonderful, but as Christmas approaches, allow yourself to dwell on the goodness that you can share with others, particularly those in need.

THE SELF ELF

Can we ever truly grasp what Jesus had to give up in order to become human and walk this earth with us? Scripture tells us that although Jesus had equality with God, he gave up his supreme entitlement to become human. We may never quite understand this act, but I think we can accept that Jesus' birth and death on the cross was our ultimate example of sacrifice.

We may be involved in the spirit of giving this season, but are we involved in the spirit of *giving up*? Are we willing to sacrifice, as in the example of Jesus, regarding others before ourselves? This is not to attribute a higher worth based on superior authority or qualities, but to understand people's value in light of Christ.

> *Do nothing from selfish ambition or conceit, but in humility regard others as better than yourselves. Let each of you look not to your own interests, but to the interests of others (Philippians 2:3-4,* NRSV*).*

Do you recognize selfish ambition in your life? Reflect on Jesus' sacrifice, and in your thankfulness, make a commitment to imitate him by seeing the good in others and pursuing their interests above your own.

DECEMBER 22

CHRISTMAS TRUCE

In the Christmas of 1914, German and British soldiers declared a Christmas truce and began a series of widespread ceasefires along the Western Front. In the week leading up to the holiday, soldiers crossed trenches and ventured into no man's land to exchange seasonal greetings and food, play football, and take part in joint burial ceremonies and prisoner swaps. The Christmas truce is seen as a symbolic moment of peace and humanity amidst one of the most violent events of human history.

The Christmas spirit is often talked of throughout this season, and while at times it seems to take away from the pure celebration of Christ, it is encouraging to read of stories where goodwill seems to conquer in the midst of a stressful and often hurtful world.

> *Let the peace of Christ rule in your hearts, since as members of one body you were called to peace (Colossians 3:15, NIV).*

Is there a time and place this Christmas for you to offer a Christmas truce? Can you set aside family differences, long-standing arguments, or even regrets, in order to create harmony? Be intentional this year—Christ may be more evident in your midst than you realize.

DECEMBER 23

STOP AND LISTEN

The Bible story of Martha and Mary is well known, and many of us feel rather empathetic toward Martha. As women, we manage many responsibilities and tasks, and it requires a lot of hard work and hospitality. This seems especially true as we approach Christmas, when our "to-do" lists grow, and events and celebrations take over our lives.

But sometimes in this season, we worry about the unnecessary things—things that will not last beyond the day. Mary chose the "good part" when Jesus was visiting. She focused on the guest, not the preparations.

> *Martha was distracted with all her preparations; and she came up to Him and said, "Lord, do You not care that my sister has left me to do all the serving alone? Then tell her to help me." But the Lord answered and said to her, "Martha, Martha, you are worried and bothered about so many things; but only one thing is necessary, for Mary has chosen the good part, which shall not be taken away from her" (Luke 10:40-42, NASB).*

Will you let the Lord show you what things are distracting you from what really matters? As you take this small moment of time to reflect on Jesus, remind yourself that this is the lasting part of your day.

DECEMBER 24

JOURNEY OF HOPE

The day had almost arrived! There were many people waiting for the birth of Jesus. The Jews had long awaited their Messiah, Mary and Joseph were waiting for their firstborn baby, and the Wise Men were looking for the sign. Jesus was the hope that they all looked toward.

There is always a journey involved in waiting for great expectations to be fulfilled. The Jews were preparing themselves for the appointed time, Mary and Joseph had to travel to another town, and the Wise Men had to follow the star. In our own lives, we sometimes forget that the journey is part of the fulfilment of the things that we hope for.

"Look, the virgin shall conceive and bear a son,
nd they shall name him Emmanuel,
which means, 'God is with us'" (Matthew 1:23, NRSV).

Are you waiting and hoping for something great to be fulfilled? Take a moment today to reflect on the journey of those that waited expectantly for their Savior. Pray that hope will remain in your heart for what is to come.

CARRY THE STORY

You will probably celebrate today with some manner of tradition. We celebrate with popular cultural traditions and also with our own particular family traditions. Whatever these traditions are, you probably hold them very near to your heart and hope they will last as time goes on.

Have you ever felt lost in all the tradition and wondered if Jesus is truly being celebrated? It's easy to feel disappointed when we forget to elevate Jesus in all of the celebrations. But remember, our celebration of this day actually serves the purpose of carrying the story of Good News forward!

> *In that region there were shepherds living in the fields, keeping watch over their flock by night. Then an angel of the Lord stood before them, and the glory of the Lord shone around them, and they were terrified. But the angel said to them, "Do not be afraid; for see—I am bringing you good news of great joy for all the people: to you is born this day in the city of David a Savior, who is the Messiah, the Lord" (Luke 2:8-11,* NRSV*).*

Let's not frown on the fact that the world seems to have commercialized this paramount event in history. Instead, let's use the festivities to our advantage. Take time today to tell the miraculous story of our Savior's birth, so that it will continue to be carried through the generations!

BOXING DAY REWARD

In many countries around the world, the day after Christmas is called Boxing Day: a tradition that began in a time when tradespeople were given Christmas boxes of money or presents to acknowledge good service throughout the year.

While we don't like to think of ourselves as servants these days, many of us are involved in employment or some type of service. The Bible says much about those that have shown diligence and respect to those who are in authority.

> *All who are under the yoke of slavery should consider their masters worthy of full respect, so that God's name and our teaching may not be slandered (1 Timothy 6:1, NIV).*

There is a higher purpose to us respecting our employers. We may not get our Boxing Day reward for recognition of our service, but we will be honoring God's name as a witness of Christian living. Be encouraged as you go back into your place of work (whether home, study, or employment), knowing that as you show good service, you are positively representing the name of Jesus.

DECEMBER 27

HIGHWAYS

If you stop to think about it, most of our conversations are made up of a dialogue of various opinions. We talk about the facts, for sure, but the meaningful stuff comes when we start to influence those facts with our own sentiments.

There's nothing wrong with searching for meaning in situations and trying to make sense of the complexities of life. It's possible that the quest for understanding is an integral part of our human nature. However, we ultimately need to surrender our understanding and opinions to God's truth.

"My thoughts are not your thoughts,
nor are your ways my ways, says the LORD.
For as the heavens are higher than the earth,
so are my ways higher than your ways
and my thoughts than your thoughts" (Isaiah 55:8-9, NRSV).

In the context of this scripture, God is speaking specifically about his mercy for his people. There are ways of God that we simply cannot understand, but we need to trust that his ways and thoughts are better. Are there certain "ways of God" that you just can't make sense of in your life? Be encouraged to surrender your thoughts in order to trust his.

DECEMBER 28

NEW EVERY MORNING

Some days it is good to reflect on exactly what God has saved us from. As a nation, Israel knew what it was to fail God time and time again. They rebelled against him and they deserved punishment; yet, God chose to redeem them, over and over again. His love for his people compelled him to show mercy.

We are not unlike the Israelites in our rebellion and turning away from God's purposes. We are also not unlike the Israelites in that God has incredible compassion for us. In sending his Son, Jesus Christ, God proved once and for all that his compassion will never fail.

Because of the LORD's great love, we are not consumed,
for his compassions never fail.
They are new every morning;
great is your faithfulness (Lamentations 3:22-23, NIV).

Why does God's compassion have to appear new every morning? Because we can barely go a day without failing. We need to be reminded of God's faithfulness so that we can turn toward him, daily. Did you fail God yesterday, or today? Thank him for his compassion every single morning, confess, and be ready to start the day new. His mercy endures!

DON'T BE ASHAMED

Have you ever tried to wade upstream through a river, or swim against a strong current? It is hard! Sometimes this is how we can feel as a Christian in a world full of unbelievers. Our modern culture is full of political correctness and accepting all beliefs, but when it comes to Christianity, it can feel like anything we say is offensive!

Paul was put in prison a number of times for offending the people of his time. He seemed to suffer gladly because he was convinced that Jesus was the Savior and that his mission was to share this good news with the world. Paul was convinced of the truth, and because of this, he was not ashamed!

I am suffering now because I tell the Good News, but I am not ashamed, because I know Jesus, the One in whom I have believed. And I am sure he is able to protect what he has trusted me with until that day (2 Timothy 1:12, NCV).

Do you tend to keep quiet about your faith in Jesus? Are you worried about suffering, or being mocked for your beliefs? Take time each day to develop your relationship with him; the more you know Jesus, the more confident you will be in what you believe. Imitate Paul's dedication to sharing the gospel and trust God to protect you.

MIND OVER MATTER

As you look toward the New Year, you will probably think about your goals and aspirations. And one of those goals is likely to exercise more! We know the value of exercise; it benefits the body and the mind. We also know that exercise requires determination and discipline.

There is, however, exercise that is more beneficial than physical exercise. Scripture compares godliness with bodily exercise. Godliness is not just something that we instantly receive when we accept Christ as our Savior. Godliness is a work in progress. It requires discipline and commitment to understanding what it means to be like Jesus.

> *Bodily exercise profits a little, but godliness is profitable for all things, having promise of the life that now is and of that which is to come (1 Timothy 4:8, NKJV).*

Do you accept that you are going to have to put in the time and effort to prioritize spiritual practices in the same way you try to with physical exercise? Godliness has benefit beyond this life. Be encouraged that you will be rewarded in both this life and the life to come!

ON THE RIGHT TRACK

What are you going to do next year? When we are experiencing the end of one year and looking toward the next, we can become overwhelmed with the need to plan what we hope to achieve. Maybe you hope to start your career, find a husband, have a child, go on a missions trip, or begin studying.

When your heart motivation for those plans is right, you need not be anxious about how you are going to make it happen. The Lord is always present to guide you in the way you should go. God also knows that plans don't happen without steps. So before you hit the ground running with your ideas, allow him to show you the next step.

> *The true children of God are those who let God's Spirit lead them (Romans 8:14, NCV).*

God will never lead you into anything you are not ready for. Ask the Lord today for his guidance in both your plans for next year and in the steps you need to take to get there. May God richly bless you as you surrender your ways to his.